PEMBROKESHIRE HUMOUR

Jokes and Anecdotes from the Celtic Fringe

Brian John

Greencroft Books

1994

CONTENTS

Typesetting: Sally Rudman and Brian John
Printing: Lewis Printers, Carmarthen
Design: Brian John using Claris Works software on Apple Mac LC475 computer

Illustrations: from Victorian children's comics and illustrated journals

Acknowledgements: I acknowledge my debt to the many Pembrokeshire people who have told their stories to me in person, over the telephone or in writing during many months of entirely frivolous research. The contributors are too numerous to mention by name, but I hope that they will be sufficiently rewarded by seeing their jokes in print.

Greencroft Books, Trefelin, Cilgwyn, Newport, Pembs SA42 OQN. Tel: 0239 - 820470

ISBN 0 905559 69 X

INTRODUCTION

Is there such a thing as Pembrokeshire Humour? I believe that there is, and that the sense of humour of Pembrokeshire people is rather special.

In this day and age jokes and anecdotes tend to be international, transmitted over the radio and television and published in newspapers, books and magazines. A joke told in a public house in Milford Haven may have come from New York or Melbourne, and it may have changed its form a hundred times on its way to Pembrokeshire. It is just as likely to be a Jewish joke as an American or English one, and it may well have been heard before, in one guise or another, by those who listen to it today and who still find it amusing.

In putting together this collection of jokes I have been amazed to find "old faithfuls" turning up in the most unexpected places. For example, the old story about Shemi Wad and the Giant Cabbage must have originated in Pembrokeshire well over a century ago, but I was greatly surprised to see it in a collection of American jokes published around 1940 -- without Shemi and featuring New Englanders and Californians boasting about the wonders of their home territories. Did the joke travel with Pembrokeshire emigrants to America in the latter years of the last century? Similarly, I have discovered virtually identical jokes in collections from Scotland and Ireland; and jokes about the legendary meanness of Cardi folk are also told about the tight-fisted folk of Aberdeen. Jokes are constantly evolving, with every good Pembrokeshire raconteur doing his bit to keep them up to date; in the same way professional television and radio comedians keep their acts fresh by recycling old favourites and giving them some local or topical slant.

But let's come back to the question of the uniqueness of Pembrokeshire humour. In my view it is simple, gentle, and free of the hard edge which characterises the humour of the slick and sophisticated urban English. If one is looking for comparisons, one can find most in common with Irish jokes or with the jokes of rural Scotland. Pembrokeshire jokes tend to be whimsical and wry, with their heroes often guilty of nothing more than a sort of twisted logic; we tend to laugh with these folk heroes, rather than at them, and we secretly admire their simplicity and their ability to look at the world from oblique angles.

I hope that the jokes on the following pages will provide some innocent amusement both for Pembrokeshire people and for visitors. It remains to say that any similarities between the persons featured in these stories and any persons living or dead are entirely coincidental! Further, I have no wish to claim any copyright in the tales recounted; very few of them are original, and if anybody wants to use any of them in another context I will be only too pleased.

Brian John — November 1994

Chapter Two

LOCAL CHARACTERS

The Flying Trousers of Twm Waunbwll

Thomas Phillips of Glandwr, near Crymych, was a famous local character in the early years of this century. In Welsh he was known as "Twm Waunbwll" after the name of his farm to the east of the little hamlet. Like Shemi Wad he was a renowned cyfarwydd, but in addition to the tall stories told by him to others, there are many tales still in local circulation about his eccentricities. He was an old bachelor who lived most of his life with his widowed mother. When he died in December 1914 there was great local sadness, for he was held in affection by the whole farming community of the Crymych area and the lower Teifi Valley.

Twm used to catch the local train (traditionally known as the "Cardi Bach") to Cardigan market every Saturday. He used to travel with a great sack into which he would dump all his weekly shopping -- meat, tea, sugar, fish, nails, candles, bread and everything else. One day, on his walk to the station at Llanglydwen to catch the train, he sat by the roadside for a little rest. Later, as he got to the station, he started to feel distinctly uncomfortable, and concluded that he must have been sitting on an ant-hill. Once he was aboard the train the itching became intolerable, and Twm decided that there was nothing for it but to take his trousers off and give them a good shake. With the train now going along at a fine pace, Twm opened the carriage window, leaned out and shook his trousers energetically to get rid of the ants. However, they filled with air and were torn from his grip. Twm and his fellow passengers watched with fascination as the trousers sailed off into the sky, receding rapidly into the distance as the train chugged on serenely towards Cardigan.

Undeterred, Twm continued into the town and did his shopping as usual, attired in hat, tweed waistcoat and jacket, black boots, and violently striped Welsh woollen long johns....

Twm Goes to Sea

It was the great day of the annual trip to the seaside (Dydd Iau Mawr in Welsh). As usual, the Glandwr families and the whole community round about set out in the early morning, piled into wagons and carts, with some on horseback.

Twm Waunbwll was in the throng, on his best pony. His Mam was in one of the wagons, determined to keep a good eye on him lest he should be led astray by his wild friends from the village. The journey to Aberporth was long and hot, and when the expedition forces arrived there Twm was not in a good humour. He was a very large young man, and the pony did not really accommodate him adequately; as a result he had a sore bum, quite apart from feeling hot and bothered. Once on the beach, he sat and sulked while all his friends went in for a swim. But then, since it would be some little time before the picnic was ready, the young men decided to hire a rowing boat and go for a trip around the bay. "Come on, Twm!" they shouted. "Don't sit there looking so miserable!" And after much cajoling, Twm was convinced to join his pals in the boat. They placed him in the stern, where his great weight had the effect of lifting the bows well clear of the water. And so, with the boat looking distinctly down-at-heel, off they went around the bay, with Twm's friends taking it in turns to row.

They all had a wonderful time, singing, shouting to the folks on the shore, and directing amiable insults at whichever incompetent rower happened to be in charge. The sea was calm and the water warm, but during the whole trip Twm sat petrified in the stern, hanging onto the sides of the boat for dear life, and not saying a word to anybody. At last, when they had all returned and were safely ashore, the lads ran laughing up the beach to where the picnic was all laid out on sheets and blankets. Twm followed, trembling and white-faced. "Well now, Twm", said his Mam as he arrived, "Did you enjoy the trip on the water?" Twm almost exploded. "Enjoy?" he said, with passion. "Enjoy? Dammo, Mam, how could I enjoy a thing like that with only half an inch of planking between me and Eternity?"

Twm and the Men from the Ministry

Shortly before Twm Waunbwll died in 1914 the country was plunged into war with Germany. There was grave concern about the country's ability to grow its own food supplies, and government surveyors were sent out to visit every farm with a view to calculating how many acres of cereals might be grown. One day two of these surveyors appeared in the Glandwr area, and Twm discovered that without his knowledge or permission they had ensconced themselves in one of his fields. They put up a tent and appeared to be turning the field into their operational HQ.

Twm was none too pleased with this development, and strode up to the tent to remonstrate with the Men from the Ministry, speaking of course in Welsh. The inspectors spoke no Welsh, and tried to explain what they were doing in English. Soon it became apparent that English was a foreign language to Twm, but all seemed to be well when the men showed Twm their official permit, printed on blue paper. Mumbling under his breath, Twm walked back up to the farm, leaving the inspectors to analyse their maps in their tent.

But Twm was not to be beaten, and he instructed one of his farm hands to move his notoriously fierce herd of Welsh Black cattle into the field where the tent was pitched. Then he climbed onto a hedge to enjoy the fun and games. As soon as the cattle saw the tent they rushed playfully towards it. The thundering hooves caused the Men from the Ministry to make a very rapid evacuation, and after trying to frighten off the animals they fled in disarray across the field with the playful cattle in hot pursuit. One of the men spotted Twm sitting on the hedge roaring with laughter. "For God's sake, man," he shouted with terror in his voice, "do something to stop them!" At this Twm cupped his hands around his mouth and yelled back (in Welsh, of course): "Show them the blue paper!"

Tommy and the Resurrection

Tommy "Ginger" James was a great local character who lived in Cosheston. He worked in Pembroke Dockyard, and after a hard day's work he would take a few jars of ale on his way home. His last watering hole en route was the Commercial Inn at Llanion. One evening, after a very heavy session at the public bar he managed to ride his bicycle part of the way home, but ran out of steam close to the cemetery gates just outside town. He parked his cycle at the gates, entered the cemetery, and found a convenient newly dug grave which was warm and dry. In he tumbled, and went fast asleep.

Next morning Tommy's mates from Cosheston came by on their way to work, and on seeing his bicycle at the cemetery gates they went inside to investigate. "Tommy! Tommy!" they shouted. "Time to get up!" Upon hearing this commotion Tommy woke up with a start, poked his head above the edge of the grave and saw that he was surrounded by tombstones. "Jesus Christ!" he said to himself. "It is the Resurrection Morning, and Tommy James is the first one up!"

Georgie's Trip to Market

In the old days it used to be said (by people who should have known better) that the people of Marloes were a bit slow on the up-take. They were referred to all over Pembrokeshire as "Marloes gulls", maybe because gull's eggs were a part of their diet. There are many famous stories about Marloes folk, and this is one of them.

Billy was out one Friday morning in his garden, dressed up in his oilskins since it was pouring with rain. He was watering his roses with a watering-can. As he worked he saw his friend Georgie going past, with a wheelbarrow half-full of onions. Later on in the day, just as it was getting dark, he saw Georgie coming back again, still pushing his wheelbarrow with the onions in it.

"Where'st tha bin?" shouted Billy.

"It's Harfat market tomorrow," replied Georgie. "Tis a devil of a long way to go with all me onions to sell, so I thought to meself I'd go halfway today, so as to make the journey that much quicker tomorrow."
"So why hast tha come back again after goin' all that way?"

"I has to get a good night's rest in me own bed so as to have the strength for the rest of the journey. An' can't tha see, tha daft bugger, that me barra is only half-full of onions? I had to come back whatever, to fetch the other half."

Billy's Sad Task

This is another tale about the good folks of Marloes. Old Josh Edwards was walking along the Martin's Haven lane one day when he noticed his friend Billy hard at work in a field. On closer examination he saw that Billy was digging a deep hole in the ground, and that there were four other holes nearby, surrounded by great piles of earth.

"Mornin' Billy," said Josh. "Big job tha's doin' there. What's tha diggin' all them holes for?"

"Mornin' Josh," replied Billy, a bit short of breath. "Bad business it is. Me ol' sheepdog have died, an' I has to bury'n. But I'm havin' terrible trouble with all this diggin'. Them two holes over by there was too big an' these two holes over by here was too small to fit the ol' dog into. I hopes to God I gets it right this time, or I'll be here all night."

There's Money in Sheep

Lenny Badd, who died a few years ago, was a well-loved local character who ran a small sheep farm on the flanks of Carningli, near Newport. According to local legend, one day while his wife was dyeing a bedspread a little molly lamb which was in the kitchen fell into the bucket of dye and emerged bright blue in colour. Lenny immediately realised its novelty value and sold it to a passing English tourist for fifty pounds. He saw that he was onto a good thing, so he dyed all his other lambs in bright colours and sold them at a vast profit to other holidaymakers. With the money he made he bought all the other lambs in Pembrokeshire, dyed them red, and green, and purple and yellow, and made even more money. And before long Lenny was the biggest lamb dyer in the whole of Wales.

The Wild Man of Skokholm

The last man to farm on Skokholm was one Jack Edwards, always known to the Marloes people as "The Bulldog". He was aptly named, being short of build and possessing immense physical strength. In his youth he was in constant trouble on account of his short temper and his tendency to solve problems with his fists. But he was also widely read, and was one of those converted during the great religious revival of 1904-1905. During his stay on the island he kept a small herd of milking cows, over one hundred hens, four pigs and various horses and fat cattle. He grew some corn and root vegetables, and he always had a good hay harvest. He sold eggs and butter on the mainland every week, and also derived an income from the sale of livestock, rabbits, seabird eggs, lobsters and crayfish.

Bulldog Edwards had a reputation as a good farmer, but he was also a hard taskmaster. Various young men and women entered his service on the island, and he always insisted that he got value for money out of them. The little story of the Wild Man of Skokholm relates to one of his farm lads who worked on the island around the year 1908.

Edward Pearce had come to Pembrokeshire from "away" or "up the line". For one so young he appears to have been something of a character, and he was reputed to be quite fearless. During his time in Marloes he was greatly admired as the only person who had ever had the courage to pinch apples from the policeman's garden. He went to work for Bulldog Edwards on Skokholm, and for three years he remained there without once returning to the mainland. When he came back to civilisation he looked like the Wild Man of Borneo, with a thick beard and long hair falling down over his shoulders. His appearance caused great amusement until he was eventually prevailed upon to have a shave and a haircut.

Young Edward, having survived the rigours of life on Skokholm for three years without a break, had a huge appetite, and it was known that he had a passion for gulls' eggs. One evening in the village inn he was asked how many eggs he could consume at one sitting and he replied that thirty would be just about right. This remark was greeted with incredulity, and one of the regulars at the bar immediately issued him a challenge, claiming that he could not possibly eat thirty hard-boiled hens' eggs. "No problem at all," said young Edward. Warming to the challenge, Charlie Hooper said "If tha ca'st eat 'em, I'll pay for 'em." Jimmy Edwards the Shop was there at the time and he immediately went and fetched thirty eggs. These were duly hard-boiled, as more and more people crowded in to see the action.

Much to everybody's astonishment, Edward sat down and happily demolished all thirty hard-boiled hens' eggs. Years later, an old man who told the story to Roscoe Howells recalled "Well now, them eggs went down one after t'other, smooth as water off a goose's back. An' dost tha know, the young bugger only had to have salt with the last ten!"

Trouble for an Amorous Bard

One day around the year 1360 Dafydd ap Gwilym came to a fine city. We do not know which city it was, but we can presume that it was Haverfordwest, not too far from his home area, growing rapidly at the time and already anglicised to the extent that Welsh travellers were treated with some suspicion. Dafydd was feeling in a good mood, so he took lodgings in "a rather high class inn" for his young servant and himself. He ordered some good quality wine, and spotted a slim and pretty girl who was "as fair as the rising sun" among the guests. Not being a man to waste time, Dafydd immediately invited the bashful girl to his table for a roast meal and a few mugs of his wine. She agreed, and one thing led to another. Dafydd became quite infatuated with the girl; he spoke two magic words to her which had the desired effect, and he promised that he would come to her bed when everybody else in the inn was asleep.

At last all was quiet, and when he was convinced that the girl and himself were the only ones still awake Dafydd embarked upon what he later called "his dreadful journey". It was a pitch black night, and there was not a single lighted candle anywhere in the inn. First of all Dafydd fell over something, making a great noise in the process. He got up, groped his way across the floor, and then fell over a stool which the landlord had carelessly left in an inconvenient place. This created more noise, but in spite of the fact that some people must by now have been awake our hero was inflamed with passion and continued towards his destination. In rising, Dafydd banged his head against the edge of the table, knocking a basin and a copper cooking pot to the floor. Temporarily stunned, he leaned against the table, inadvertently pushing aside one of the trestles so that the whole table collapsed. There was an almighty racket as pots, pans, dishes, cutlery and beer mugs all crashed to the floor, waking up every person in the inn and causing the innkeeper's dogs to start barking as if the end of the world was at hand.

By now three Englishmen named Hickin, Jenkin and Jack, who lay "in a smelly bed next to the high walls", were wide awake, and quite convinced that Dafydd was up to no good. "There's a sneaky Welshman prowling about here," spluttered Jenkin, "and he's up to no good. He'll rob us if he can. He's a thief. Be on your guard!" And they grabbed their packs and stared into the darkness as Dafydd tried to hide. Now pandemonium reigned. The landlord roused everybody in the inn, lighting candles to assist in the search for the unknown criminal. Dafydd hid himself away silently in a dark corner while the search parties ranged high and low, and prayed "passionately from the heart". At last, by the grace of Jesus or through sheer good luck, he found the opportunity to return to the sanctuary of his own bed, and dived beneath the covers while the commotion died down.

For the rest of the night he lay wide awake, battered and bruised, and (according to the old poem) thanking the saints for their intervention and begging God for forgiveness. No doubt the bright young girl with the black hair lay wide awake too, thinking her own very private thoughts......

Shemi's Wager

It was a thirsty night in Goodwick, and the inns were doing a roaring trade. There was talk, and laughter, and dim lights, with ale spilling onto the sawdust floors with increasing frequency as the night wore on. Shemi Wad was in the Rose and Crown, greatly enjoying himself. The talk turned to the drinking abilities of those present at the bar, and there was a bit of an argument. Somebody challenged Shemi that he couldn't drink eight pints of ale on the trot. Shemi was not a man to pass up a challenge, and so a wager was made. Two gold sovereigns were deposited with the innkeeper, and a time was fixed for the contest the next evening. The betting was fast and furious, as the Rose and Crown regulars assessed Shemi's drinking abilities and put down their money on the outcome of the contest.

Next evening a great crowd assembled in the Rose and Crown at the appointed time. The pint pots were made ready, and more money changed hands as the men waited for Shemi to turn up for the fray. But Shemi did not appear. At last some of the regulars started to mock Shemi, claiming that he had turned yellow and had ducked out of the contest. Laughter began to echo around the bar.

But much later in the evening, with the contest time long since past, Shemi appeared at the door. "Come on, Shemi!" shouted one. "Shame on you, Shemi!" shouted another. "Have you given in then? Is eight pints too many?" The bar became quiet as the men all waited for Shemi's reply.

"No, No, boys bach," replied Shemi, after a theatrical pause. "Eight pints is no problem. I've just been in the Hope and Anchor next door, getting in a good bit of practice. Now I'm ready. Where are those eight pint pots, then?"

A Voice from Heaven

Hugh Foster was larger than life in more senses than one -- a warm and friendly man with a taste for eccentric challenges. He bought Castell Henllys, an Iron Age hill-fort near Meline, and for some years followed his dream of reconstructing some of the ancient round-houses on the site and opening them to the public. To promote his enterprise he frequently dressed in authentic Iron Age chieftain's garb, and armed with shield and spear he would turn up in Newport to do his shopping in the local supermarket. This never failed to amaze the tourists, since Hugh was a mighty man, well over six feet tall and weighing in excess of twenty stones. When he moved the earth shook and the cameras clicked......

The community was shocked when Hugh died suddenly in 1991. About a fortnight after the funeral service had been held a friend had occasion to ring the family home at Castell Henllys in order to pass on his condolences to Mrs Foster. He was somewhat taken aback when, instead of hearing a female voice at the other end, he heard the following words from the family ansafone: "I am very sorry that I am not here to take your call just now. If you would like to leave your name and telephone number after the bleep I will get in touch with you just as soon as I can."

The voice was unmistakably that of Hugh, presumably using a direct line from Heaven............

The Poor Old Devil

One of the great local characters of Haverfordwest in the last century was one John Morgan, a builder who lived in Prendergast. He took his trade very seriously (building, for example, the tower on Haverfordwest Castle and many of the limestone buildings of Pembroke Dockyard) but he derived most satisfaction in life from carrying on the work of God. Although he was untrained as a minister, he worked tirelessly in Prendergast to combat poverty and to bring religion to the people.

John preached and campaigned at every opportunity; he started a Baptist Sunday School for children; he initiated a 7 am Sunday morning prayer meeting for the sleepy folks of Prendergast and personally woke up the faithful at 6 am so as to make sure they would attend; he started a clothing club and a savings bank; and very often he would walk 15 miles or more after work in the evening just to attend a prayer meeting in some distant chapel in rural Pembrokeshire. When his men were working at Pembroke Dockyard the gates were opened at 6 am, but early arrivals often found John Morgan on his soap-box preaching the gospel in the thin light of dawn.

So great was John's influence in the tight little community of Prendergast that the efforts of the local Rector and other ministers appeared paltry by comparison. On one occasion a local man was heard to remark: "The poor old Devil used to walk up Prendergast Hill with his hands in his pockets, thinkin' that the territory was all his own. But now the poor bugger has got to get through like greased lightnin' afore Johnny Morgan catches up with'n!"

Chapter Three

TALL TALES

King Arthur's Last Act

King Arthur was very old, and he came to Pembrokeshire to die. With his great sword Excalibur at his side, he lay in a small cottage in Bosherston, not far from the place where his old friend Gawain had made his hermit's cell. He was fading fast, and around him were gathered the last of the Knights of the Round Table, also very old and frail.

"My lord, is there anything you want?" asked the grey-haired Sir Launcelot. "Speak, and it shall be yours."

"No, no," replied the dying king. "Just sit me up on my pillow and open the window, so that I may smell the mayflower and the salt breeze from the sea." So they did as he asked.

"Now then, dear friend," he said to the aged Sir Galahad, "hand me my mighty Excalibur, which has served me so well over all these years in my quests and my battles." So Galahad limped to the bedside and put the great sword into the King's hand.

Arthur raised the sword high and summoned up the last of his strength, sitting upright in the bed and facing the open window. "Farewell, my good and true comrades," he whispered. "I shall cast my sword to the wind. Wherever it lands, bury me there." And with his last gasp he threw it with all his might.

So they buried him on top of the wardrobe.

Tom Birch's Tall Tales

Tom Birch was one of the most eccentric characters of Haverfordwest, who owned a tailor's shop near the bottom of High Street in the early years of this century. He ran the business with considerable enterprise and great good humour, assisted by a resourceful travelling salesman who was well known throughout Pembrokeshire.

Tom was a great teller of tall tales, and spent much of his time in his shop either inventing new and outrageous stories or recounting them to incredulous listeners. Tom loved the seaside, and often travelled to Broad Haven or Newgale during the summer months. Once upon a time, he told his cronies with due solemnity, he went down to "The Haven" for a swim. It was a very hot summer's day, and the water was calm and warm. He had a good swim, and decided that before swimming back to the shore he would have a rest by floating on his back. While in this position he fell asleep, and when he woke up he was amazed to discover that a seagull had laid an egg on his chest.

On another occasion Tom was on a cycling trip to Newgale. It was a fine summer's day, but as Tom looked out to sea he could see the rain clouds gathering. He decided that it was going to rain before long, so he jumped on his bicycle and headed for home. He looked back and could see the rain coming in over the beach at Newgale. But he was determined to keep ahead of the rain, and pedalled so quickly and travelled so fast that when he got home his front wheel was quite dry and only his back mudguard was wet.

When the weather was hot Tom enjoyed going down to the river bank near the New Bridge to eat his sandwiches at lunch-time. One day after a hard morning in the shop Tom ate his sandwiches and fell fast asleep in the sun. The tide had been low at the time. He did not know how long he had been asleep, but when he woke up he discovered that he was in Neyland. Honest to goodness,the tide had come up the river and picked him up, fast asleep. Then it had gone out again, carrying him down stream on the ebb all the way to Neyland.

Shemi and the Boat

Shemi Wad of Goodwick was proud of his prowess as an inshore fisherman, and for a while he owned a small fishing boat. He also had half-shares in a fishing net with his friend Dai Reynolds. The two men used to catch mackerel, lobsters and crabs out in Fishguard Bay. One day they were fishing around the Cow and Calf Rocks off Pencaer, having enjoyed a few pints before setting off. Dai started to complain that Shemi had been taking too large a part of the catch in recent weeks, since the net was owned fifty-fifty. Shemi pretended not to hear, but when Dai persisted with his complaints he replied impatiently "If you don't shut up, Dai, I'll share this boat with you too! I'll have the inside and you can have the outside!"

No Trouble At All

Shemi Gruffydd of Efailwen was in Narberth doing his shopping, when he lost a threepenny bit. Being careful with his money, he knew all the details. He called in at the local police station to report the loss. "Come to report a lost coin, I have," said Shemi. "Quite a nice threepenny bit, date 1923, stained on the King's head and bit o' damage on the edge. I thinks I lost it on the street down by the grocer's shop. Grateful I'll be if you can report it to me if anybody finds it."

The police dutifully wrote down the details, and Shemi promised to call in on his next visit to town to see if the coin had been found.

A fortnight later Shemi came to Narberth again to do his shopping, and found that the main street had been dug up. There were men with shovels, trenches and piles of broken asphalt all over the place where the roadway had been. He called in at the police station and reported to the duty sergeant. "I see that ye've bin lookin' for me threepenny bit," he said. "Most grateful I am for all yer trouble. Have ye found it yet?"

A Sign of Good Breeding

An Englishman, a Scot and an Irishman and Madoc Jones from Crymych were discussing ancestry and good breeding. "My ancestors," said the Scot, "have faithfully taken dinner at six o'clock since the Battle of Bannockburn."

"My ancestors," said the Englishman, "have without fail dined at eight o'clock ever since the Norman Conquest."

"My ancestors," said the Irishman, "have regularly feasted at nine-thirty since the dawn of the Iron Age."

"Duw, Duw, boys bach", said Madoc "I don't like to boast, but there's many a time my old ancestors didn't take any dinner till the next day."

A Case of the Sunstroke

Evans the Post was on holiday, and since the weather was glorious he spent the whole day lying in the sun on Newgale beach. This was not very wise, since he was not at all used to the sun and normally never exposed himself. He returned to Wolfscastle after his day out, and installed himself at the bar of the Wolfe Inn. He drank ten pints of bitter, and the barman thought it a bit odd when he complained about not being able to cool down after his day in the sun. The locals decided that he was probably suffering from the sunstroke.

Suddenly an ambulance went roaring past, lights blazing and siren blaring. Evans rushed out of the door and ran after the ambulance, going full pelt down the road towards Treffgarne. As he ran he waved his arms in the air and shouted "Stop! Stop!" He began to tire at Nant-y-Coy Mill as the ambulance disappeared round the corner. "All right, you miserable sods!" he shouted. "If the colour of my money isn't good enough for you, you can keep your bloody ice-cream!"

A Stroke of Genius

Einstein Edwards was, by Marloes standards, a very smart young fellow, and the locals thought he would go far. Then somebody recommended him for an appearance on "Brain of Britain" on the BBC radio, and the whole village was delighted when he was accepted. On the great day everybody in Marloes tuned in to Radio Four, and there was great excitement when Einstein's turn came. "Now then Mr Edwards," said Robert Robinson. "What is the equinox?"

"Ah yes," said Einstein. "I thinks I knows the answer. This is a very scientific question, isn't it?"

"You could say that," said Robert Robinson.

"This is all to do with this trendy stuff about genetic engineering," said Einstein. "Therefore I has to conclude that the equinox is the strange lookin' beast produced by the crossin' of a horse with a cow."

Careful Diagnosis

An elderly gentleman named Albert was having trouble with his eyes. His GP referred him to the eye specialist at Withybush Hospital, but the waiting list was something terrible, and the trouble got worse. Then a friend told him that there was a very good Alternative Therapy clinic in Fishguard, and suggested that he should try and get a diagnosis there.

Old Albert duly made an appointment, and called in at the clinic, where he was met by a charming young lady herbalist. For a long time she discussed his medical history, explained all about holistic healing, and examined his eyes. Then she said "Now then, Albert, I am quite convinced you've got piles. Drink a teaspoon of this herbal essence three times a day. That will be ten pounds."

Albert did not get very much better, but after a few months he got his appointment with the high-powered eye specialist at Withybush. "What seems to be the trouble?" said the man in a white coat. "Well, doctor," replied Albert. "I've got this trouble with the old eyes. But there's confused I am, because when I went to see the young lady in Fishguard she looked at me eyes and said I'd got the piles."

"We had better get to the bottom of this," said the eye specialist. "Take down your trousers, so that I can have a good look." Albert obeyed, and for a long time the doctor examined his nether regions. After making copious notes he said at last: "Right, you can pull your trousers up now. I have to tell you, sir, after a detailed study of the symptoms, that you are suffering from cataract of the left eye."

New-fangled Technology

Around the beginning of the century the Constable Freddie Jenkins of Uzmaston received a bulky envelope from Police HQ. It contained a note about a notorious criminal who was thought to be at large in the area, having just escaped from Haverfordwest Goal. And being very up-to-date with new-fangled technology, the HQ staff had enclosed six photographs of the criminal, each one taken from a different angle.

Constable Jenkins was not too good at reading, so he did not absorb all the details of the police circular. But he was an enthusiastic fellow, very keen to impress and to advance his career; and he was greatly excited at the prospect of a man-hunt on his patch.

A few days later a messenger delivered the following to the Chief Constable in Haverfordwest:

"Dear Chief,

I am not too good at the writing, so Mrs Absalom the Bread is putting this down for me. She writes very good, so I hear. I have captured five of the criminals, and Mr Evans Big House has got them locked up in his cellar. I am hot on the trail of the sixth criminal. I have him under observation down by the river, and expect to arrest him any time now. Please send reinforcements since he is bigger than I am.

Yours etc,

Constable F. Jenkins."

Tall Tale from Goodwick

Shemi Wad (James Wade) of Goodwick, who died in 1887, was a renowned story teller or cyfarwydd. His tales were tall rather than short. This is one of them, recounted by Shemi himself and then told and retold a thousand times by others in the inns of Fishguard and Goodwick.

Shemi had gone fishing down on the Parrog, the broad expanse of marsh and sand-dunes between the two towns. His strong fishing-line was in the water, with a dozen hooks all baited, waiting for the fish to bite. It was a hot afternoon and Shemi felt sleepy, so he retreated up the bank, first tying the line around his waist and then nodding off to sleep on the warm flank of a sand-dune. While he slept the tide went out, and since no fish had been biting the baits were all exposed on the mud-flats. The seagulls liked the look of them and swallowed the lot - hook, line and sinker. Then something disturbed the gulls and the whole flock took off, carrying Shemi with them, still fast asleep. They flew all the way across St George's Channel, landing at last in Dublin's Phoenix Park.

In due course Shemi woke up to find himself, in the failing light, in strange surroundings. He realised he was in Ireland, and feeling somewhat concerned about his safety in this strange land he looked for somewhere to hide. Around the edges of the Park he saw a gallery of large guns. Here was the answer, thought Shemi - and he slipped into the barrel of a cannon and went off to sleep. He did not know that a salute was fired from the guns every morning;

and so it was that the still sleeping Shemi was shot out of the gun barrel, to fly straight back across St George's Channel. As luck would have it, he landed on the soft green grass of Pencw, right above his home.

Afterwards Shemi swore blind that every detail of the story was true, and all his listeners swore blind that they believed him.....

Using the System

Aneurin Ty Glas was an old farmer who lived in a remote spot up on Dinas Mountain. One day the pilot of the National Park Spying Helicopter looked down from on high and saw that a beautiful new building was being erected on the edge of Aneurin's farmyard. Within twenty-four hours Evil Evans, the National Park Enforcement Officer, was knocking on Aneurin's door at Ty Glas. "Good day to you, sir!" said Evil. "It appears that you are building a large building in the corner of your farmyard, and to the best of my knowledge it does not have planning permission. May I ask what it is you are building?"

"I was wonderin' when you was goin' to turn up," said Aneurin. "None of your bloody business, if you asks me. But since you asks, I'll tell you. If I can let it, it's a cow-shed, and if I can't let it it's a medieval ruin. Bad shape it is in, to be sure, and it will sure as eggs fall on my head if I don't do somethin' about it. And if you wants me to take it down you've got another thing comin', Sonny Jim, since I've bin workin' on it these twenty years and me grandpa has bin livin' in it ever since he passed his eightieth birthday, some fifteen years back."

Tenby's Wonderful Machine

Tenby has a reputation for being in the forefront of modern technology when it comes to the amusement of tourists. Not long ago Tony Eldorado, one of the enterprising businessmen of the town, installed a machine in his amusement arcade which would give the correct answer to any question after you put 50p in the slot.

On the great day for the inauguration of the machine Tony invited all the civic dignitaries of the town around for a demonstration. "Ladies and gentlemen," he said proudly. "This machine is the latest thing from Japan. It will attract thousands of visitors and transform the economy of this seaside town, and I am proud to be the person responsible. Now then, let me give a demonstration."

So he put 50p in the slot and asked a simple question. "Where is my father now?" he asked. "Your father is fishing from the harbour wall in Saundersfoot," replied the machine. The civic dignitaries were not impressed, because they thought, like Tony, that his father was dead. So Tony rephrased his question:

"Where is my mother's husband?"

Back came the reply: "Your mother's husband is buried in Pembroke Dock, but your father is still fishing from the harbour wall in Saundersfoot."

Cause for Celebration

Melfyn and his wife Teleri lived in a little hovel up in the hills near Morfil. Teleri was heavy with child, and one dark winter's night she went into labour. Melfyn rushed out and got the doctor, and they got back to the house just in time. The doctor ran into the little bedroom where Teleri lay, and in the dim light he asked Melfyn to bring the lamp closer as he helped with the birth. At last he said "Melfyn, you are the proud father of a little boy."

"Wonderful!" said Melfyn. "Let me pop over to the cupboard, and we'll all share a little drink."

"Just a minute," replied the doctor. "Hold the light a little closer. Ah yes, as I thought -- you're the proud father of twins."

"Amazing!" said Melfyn. "This calls for us to open a bottle."

"Wait, wait," the doctor said. "Come and hold the light a little closer. Congratulations, you're the father of triplets."

"I can hardly believe it," murmured Melfyn, feeling faint. "We'd better have a bottle each."

"Not just yet," said the doctor. "Hold the light a little closer."

"I don't want to be difficult," groaned Melfyn, "but do you think this bloody light's attracting them?"

Money Management

Tommy Mathias from Freystrop was new to bank accounts, and had a bit of trouble learning all the ins and outs of using cheques instead of real money. The bank manager in Haverfordwest told Tommy that he must look after his brand new cheque book very carefully, so he was very worried when he lost it in the middle of the crowd of shoppers in Bridge Street one Saturday morning.

Tommy went back to the bank on the following Monday to report the loss to the bank manager. "In me pocket one minute, it was," he explained, "but next minute gone, in front of Charlie Cook Butchers. And not a single cheque used up. So I've come to have a new one with you."

"Oh dear," said the bank manager. "This is very serious. Have you reported the loss to the police?"

"No no," replied Tommy. "No need for that. I ain't so stupid as I looks. Nobody else can use me cheques, since I made sure to sign every one of them meself as soon as I had the cheque book the other day."

Mistaken Identity

An American tourist went into the Royal Oak inn in Fishguard to absorb a bit of the local atmosphere. He went to the bar for a pint of ale, and struck up a conversation with Willy Williams, who happened to have a very large Irish wolfhound sitting next to him. "Good day to you, sir!" said the American. "Say, does your dog bite?"

"Not at all," said Willy. "My dog is gentle as a lamb. Never bit anybody in his life."

So the American went over and patted the Irish wolfhound on the head, upon which the dog snarled ferociously, bit his arm and flung him to the floor.

Picking himself up gingerly, the American shouted "I thought you told me your dog didn't bite?"

"Quite right you are," replied Willy. "My dog is called Fido, and he's back home on the mat in front of the fire. This dog by here is called Rambo, and he belongs to Johnny Jenkins who's just gone to have a pee."

Shemi Goes Fishing

Shemi Wad liked to tell how he had once caught a giant herring when he was out with the nets. It weighed no less than four and twenty stones, and Shemi and Dai couldn't get it into their boat. So they towed it to Old Beach and dragged it up on the pebbles. When they opened up the monster fish they were greatly surprised to find Jonah inside, alive and kicking and grateful to be rescued.

On another occasion Shemi was fishing with a line from the river bank in the Cwm. He caught a fine sewin, and he was pulling it in when along came a great big heron from nowhere. The bird swallowed the sewin and the hook, leaving Shemi hanging onto the line for dear life. He tried to pull the heron in to the bank, but the old bird was so strong that it flew off out to sea, with Shemi dragged along behind. High above the clouds they flew. Once or twice the bird began to tire, and flew lower and lower until Shemi was in danger of falling into the sea; but our hero helped out by flapping his arms and legs in order to gain height again. At last the heron landed, and Shemi came down with a bump on a big rock by the sea-side. He landed so hard that his feet made deep marks on the rock. He realised that he was in Ireland, and was wondering what to do next when a giant crab came along. Shemi immediately leaped onto its back, and off it swam towards Pembrokeshire again, delivering the intrepid fisherman safely back to Goodwick. The poor old crab died from its exertions, and gave a good solid meal to Shemi and half the village. Then he used the crab's shell to make a nice new roof for his pig-sty.

The Pennar Businessman

Shane was a young man from Pennar who tired of looking for a job and decided at last to go it alone as a businessman. He convinced his bank manager to lend him £1000, and embarked upon his business enterprise. A fortnight later he called in to see his bank manager again, and asked for a further £1000 loan.

"I think we'd better have a little talk about this," said the bank manager. "Tell me, what have you done with the first thousand pounds?"

"Well," said Shane, "I bought a tractor for £1000, traded it for two cars, traded each of them for two motorbikes, swapped each of the motorbikes for four mountain bikes, and then sold the whole lot for £500."

"But you didn't even make a profit," exclaimed the bank manager. "In fact, after adding in your costs you have probably lost the whole thousand pounds."

"Quite right," said Shane, "but look at all the business I did!"

Getting Insured

Old Caleb Tomos from Little Newcastle was convinced by an eager young man on his front doorstep that he ought to get himself insured. The young man promised him that he only needed to pay £2 per week for a most splendid insurance policy which would enable him to sleep easy in his bed without a single worry for the rest of his life.

Having been left a rather complicated form to fill in, Caleb settled down that night after the milking, gazing at the forbidding document in a bright pool of light cast by his paraffin lamp. He was required to fill in all sorts of things about the life, death and medical history of his parents and brothers and sisters, and thought to himself that there was not a lot he could remember after all these years. After much thought, and vaguely aware that family medical history might have some effect on his premiums, he wrote the following:

"Mother: died in infancy so far as I knows.
Father: went to bed feeling quite well and next morning woke up dead.
Brother: Albert, who was an infant, died when he was a mere child.
Sister: Daisy dropped down dead very sudden but the doctor said it was nothing serious.
Self: I have never been fatally sick in my life."

Off to London Town

Morgan Morgan from Henry's Moat went off to London to seek his fortune. Before he went his old Dad said to him: "Come back when you are nice and rich, there's a good lad. Never been to London myself, mind, but I do hear that the streets is paved with gold and all you has to do is bend over and pick it up."

When Morgan got off the train at Paddington on Sunday evening, he saw a fifty pound note lying on the platform. He picked it up and examined it carefully, for he had never seen such a thing before. "Duw Duw," he said to himself, "there's money there is in this place."

Then he threw it down onto the ground again, and said: "Mustn't be greedy, and it is after all a Sunday. One must respect the Sabbath, so I'll start to collect up the money tomorrow morning."

The Wrong Body

Once upon a time a body was washed up on the beach at Newgale. The local police constable was called to the scene, and somebody thought that the corpse might be that of Beynon Brown, an old recluse who lived in Roch. So the policeman travelled to Roch to check out the theory, and knocked on the door of Beynon's cottage.

Much to his surprise, Beynon himself opened the door. Covered in confusion, the policeman blurted out: "Good evening, sir. Sad to say, a body has been washed up on Newgale beach. Somebody thought it might be yours, so I came over to check."

"Dear me. Bad business," said Beynon. "What did the corpse look like?"

"Oh, about your height and build," replied the policeman.

"And was he wearing corduroy trousers?" asked the old man.

"Actually he was," came the reply.

"And were they brown?"

"No no. I particularly noticed that they were blue."

"Well, that settles it," said Beynon with an air of finality. "The body couldn't have been mine, because I never, never wears blue trousers."

Not Much Use

Tommy Pantglas, Aeron Tynewydd and Ianto Felinfach were ensconced by the fireside in their local inn in Maenclochog. They had had a hard day. As on many other days, they had set off with their horses and gambos before dawn to fetch loads of slaked lime for their fields, from the lime kilns near Ludchurch. Now, having travelled via Crinow Flats and Narberth, they had unloaded their gambos and stabled their horses, and they felt that they deserved a few mugs of ale.

"Evenin' boys," said Jones Grocer. "Had a good day, have you?"

"Quite good indeed, thank you, Mr Jones bach," said Tommy.

"Anything interesting happening down Ludchurch way?"

"All very quiet indeed," said Aeron, "apart from a bit of commotion on Crinow Flats."

"Oh, what was that then?" asked Jones Grocer.

"Nothin' to make a fuss about," said Ianto. "Terrible weather it was, when we was crossin' Crinow Flats, big black clouds an' bucketin' rain an' blowin' a gale. I was all huddled up an' couldn't see hardly nothin' for the rain. Then I heard this shoutin' an' yellin', an' the old gambo rocked about a bit. Thought we had gone over a big stone, I did. But the ol' horse kept goin' so I thought nothin' more of it. But then after half an hour I thought the wheel was stickin' a bit, so I got down to investigate."

"And what did you find?" asked Jones Grocer.

"Just a man's leg with a hob-nailed boot on it," replied Ianto. "But it was only a size eight, so seein' as it was not much use to me or the other boys, I chucked it away an' we carried on to fetch the lime."

A Slight Mistake

Until quite recent times there was a tall chimney stack near the County Hospital up at the top end of Haverfordwest. It could be seen for miles, and became a famous local landmark. It was built by Willy and Billy Williams, brothers who were new to the building trade but who put in a very good price for the job.

Having won the contract up at the County Hospital, they set to work with gusto. After a couple of weeks there they were, hundreds of feet up in the air on top of the chimney stack, having put the last brick in place. They sat back to enjoy their lunch, and as Willy looked out over the panorama of Haverfordwest stretched below him, Billy took out the plan and wrote on the bottom "Built very well indeed."

He passed the plan to his brother, who looked it over for a last time and then let out a yell that could be heard in Prendergast and Portfield. "Billy! Tha daft bugger!" he shouted. " Tha knows where it says "Build Well" on that contract we has with the Council? An' we though they simply wanted us to do a good job? Well, it meant what it said. We've gone an' read the bloody plan the wrong way up!"

Chapter Four

EVERYDAY LIFE

Sam's Apples

Sam Thomas had a little farm near Camrose, and he made a few extra pounds each year by selling apples from the old orchard behind the house. During the drive for extra productivity during the Second World War a man from the Ministry arrived to give Sam some advice.

"My dear Mr Thomas," said the official, "the production methods in your orchard are all very out-of-date. Fruit growing has made great strides in recent years, you know. Look here at this tree. It's not properly pruned, not properly fertilized, and it's planted in the wrong place. It must be sprayed at once, or it will die from disease. I'll be surprised if you get ten pounds of apples off this tree in the autumn."

"So will I," replied Sam. "It's a pear tree."

Tony's Wonderful Pig

An English visitor was on holiday in Begelly with his family. Next door to the holiday cottage there was a farm, and the Englishman was intrigued to see that one of the pigs in the farmyard had a wooden leg. At last he could not contain his curiosity any longer, and went to ask the farmer about the pig.

"Well now," replied Tony the farmer, "that pig is a very remarkable animal. One night when we were all asleep, the house caught fire, and the pig woke us all up and got us out of our beds, and then put out the fire. A few months ago he was out digging in the field, and he discovered a seam of coal which has brought me in a small fortune. And just now he's taking a course in Business Management at the Pembrokeshire College."

"Quite amazing," said the English visitor. "But why the wooden leg?"

"Good God!" said the farmer. "You don't expect me to eat a pig like that all in one go, do you?"

How to Lose an Election

One of the best-known figures in Pembrokeshire in the period 1950 - 1970 was Mr W.L. Davies. He was born in Tegryn, but after service in World War I he emigrated to Canada and made his fortune there in the metalworking industry. He was also a successful farmer, having operated a farm of 800 acres in New York State. He became a specialist in the manufacture of roller skates, and after returning to Britain in 1938 he eventually found his way back to Pembrokeshire and set up the Davies Roller Skates Factory in Pembroke Dock.

In 1942 "W.L" acquired Pantyderi Farm near Eglwyswrw, as well as a number of adjoining farms, and he founded Pantyderi Estates Ltd. With its 768 acres of clean land the Estate became a centre of farming innovation, and attracted a great deal of attention from the farming community throughout West Wales.

In 1955 the great man decided to stand for Parliament as an Independent candidate, having already been much involved in public life. During the election campaign one of his friends who was doing some canvassing on his behalf called on a farmer near Boncath. He spent some time extolling the virtues of the candidate, and ended his elegant speech thus:

"So, Mr Thomas bach, you can see that William Lewis Davies is the man to represent Pembrokeshire in Parliament. There are three reasons why you should vote for him. First, he is a great man, a successful industrialist and farmer, who has come home from the New World to serve Pembrokeshire faithfully and well over the years. Second, he is a local man, born and bred in these parts. And third, you and he were at school together."

"Indeed we were," came the reply, quick as a flash. "And the bugger pinched my marbles!"

Coping with Change

A well-known District Councillor named Selwyn Johns was retiring from public life after representing a small Pembrokeshire town for twenty years. On the day of his retirement the reporter from the "Tivyside Advertiser" conducted a long interview with Selwyn.

"Now then, Mr Johns," said the young lady. "You have had a long and illustrious career as a representative of the town and as guardian of its interests. You have no doubt struggled to find new jobs for the community, to improve facilities, and to clean up the environment. I suppose you have seen a great many changes in your time?"

"Indeed I has, young lady," replied the esteemed councillor. "And I've fought tooth and nail agin every single one of 'em!"

Democracy in Action

Shortly after Nicholas Bennett was elected as MP for Pembrokeshire, a deputation from Milford Haven visited him in the House of Commons. He was showing them round the Library when one of the deputation said to him "Now then, young man. I has to say to thee that the locals is not amused. Nobody knows what th'art doin' here in Westminster on behalf o' local interests. We sees nothin' in "The Telegraph" about no speeches nor nothin'. What art tha gettin' up to all the time?"

The Member for Pembroke went to a library shelf and took down a heavy tome. Then he said; "You need not worry, Mr Thomas. I take a full and active life in the Mother of Parliaments. Committees, meetings, debates, all day and all night. You see this heavy book I have in my hand? It is called Hansard, and it records all the proceedings of the House. My activities are fully recorded here. You see this page, for example? The Prime Minister's speech of March 23rd. Here, in the middle of the transcript, you see in brackets the word "Murmurs." Well, I was the man who murmured."

The Good Lord and the Potato Patch

Before his elevation to the peerage, Lord Gordon Parry lived for many years in the little town of Neyland, on the north shore of Milford Haven. He was very active in local politics, and stood in a number of parliamentary elections as a Labour candidate. He worked in Sir Thomas Picton School in Haverfordwest, and was - and still is - a very popular figure in the public life of the county.

Gordon was still living in his unpretentious terrace house in Neyland at the time of his elevation, and it took a little time for everybody to get used to his new title. According to legend, a few days after the announcement, there was an evangelical crusade going on in Neyland. A band of enthusiastic amateur evangelists had been trained in doorstep crusading techniques, and off they went on their heavenly mission. One enthusiastic young man had been briefed to knock on all the doors in the street where Lord and Lady Parry lived, in order to spread the Gospel. When he knocked on the door in question, it was opened by Lady Parry, who did not happen to be wearing her regalia at the time. Indeed, she looked, to all intents and purposes, like a perfectly ordinary housewife. The young man offered up a silent prayer, took a deep breath, and with one hand on his heart and the other on his Bible, he asked in his best trembling evangelical voice: "Madam, is the Lord in your house?"

Quick as a flash, Lady Parry replied "Not just now. He's out the back digging up some spuds. Hang on and I'll go and fetch him!"

The Tory Voter in Hakin

Old Tommy Jenkins had been a Labour voter all his life, and a faithful member of the Trade Union into the bargain. There was a parliamentary election in the offing, and the party faithful sorely missed Tommy's help on the campaign trail. But he was seriously ill, and the word went about that he was going downhill fast.
On the day before the election a rumour reached Party HQ that old Tommy had

joined the Tory Party. This was greeted with disbelief, for nobody could believe that Tommy had undergone a deathbed conversion after devoting most of his life to the Labour cause. Tommy's pals decided that severe damage was likely to be done to party morale unless this rumour could be stopped; and so a delegation was sent to visit him and find out the truth.

On arrival at Tommy's house later that evening the friends were ushered upstairs to find the old man looking very ill indeed. After a while they asked him if it was true that he had joined the Tory Party, and they were dismayed when he told them that it was indeed true. "But this is how I sees it, boys," said Tommy. "I knows my time has come, and I won't be seein' the light of day tomorrow. So there will be no vote from me in this 'ere election. But we needs every vote we can get, so I thought it was better for them buggers to lose a vote than for us to lose one of ours!"

Duly impressed by this impeccable logic, the friends departed, leaving Tommy on his death-bed with a saintly smile upon his face.

The Art of Planning

Gwynfor Murphy was a good and loyal Welshman who happened to have had an Irish grandfather. He lived on a smallholding near Fishguard with his wife Betty and one-year-old daughter during the Second World War.

Gwynfor was called up for military service, and eventually found himself in North Africa with the British Army under the leadership of Field Marshal Montgomery. He and Betty exchanged letters quite frequently, and he became quite upset when he realised that Betty could not manage the smallholding on her own. In one letter in the spring of 1943 she complained that with the baby to look after she could not possibly cope with the weeds in their large vegetable garden. Gwynfor pondered on this problem for some time, and then he had an inspiration.

He knew that all letters sent from the front were opened and vetted, and he decided to take advantage of his Irish ancestry. He wrote a long and loving letter to Betty, and added at the end: "PS. Now that the spring has come, for goodness sake don't dig the vegetable garden -- that's where the guns are."
Two or three weeks later Betty received the letter, and was somewhat mystified by the postscript. Then, early one morning, three lorry-loads of soldiers arrived and poured into her garden, armed with shovels and picks. She was not allowed to leave the house, but as she watched from an upstairs window she was amazed to see the soldiers remove every trace of weeds and then dig over her vegetable garden from one end to the other, not leaving a single square inch unturned. Eventually, disgusted and disgruntled, the soldiers returned to their lorries and roared off into the distance.

A few days later Betty received another loving letter from Gwynfor. At the end of it was a postscript which said: "Hope the chaps made a good job of digging over the garden. Don't forget to plant the spuds."

Advanced Comprehension

This is a tale from the Primary School of Herbrandston, not far from Milford Haven. One day the teacher was conducting an English lesson. In the course of it he asked the class to write down sentences with certain phrases in them.

"Now then, children," he said. "I want you to complete some sentences in an interesting way, using phrases like "as straight as an arrow", or "as tall as a tree", or "as white as a snowflake." For example, can anybody complete this sentence?"

And he wrote onto the blackboard the words "........ as hard as a ...."

Immediately Billy Jenkins shot his hand up. "Please sir! Please sir!" he said. "I knows the answer!" And he delivered his written text to the front of the classroom. The teacher examined it with interest, for it read as follows: "Tommy fell down and hurt his knee. So a ran home as hard as a could."

A Matter of Urgency

Dumpy Mathias was a young man who lived in Marloes. Since leaving school at a very early age, he had worked on a local farm, but he found that all that thinking did not agree with him, so he took a job with a local painter and decorator instead. His new boss set him to work with a big bucket of whitewash, painting the walls of a big house in the village.

A couple of hours later Dumpy's new boss called by to see how he was getting on, and found him working flat out, covered with whitewash from head to toe, and hardly stopping to draw breath. "Slow down a bit!" said the boss. "It's not natural to work that fast, and you can't possibly keep it up all day."

"Aw, I knows that, boss," replied Dumpy, puffing and panting as he slapped on another brush of whitewash. "But me whitewash in the bucket is goin' down fast, an' I has to finish this 'ere wall quick, afore it's all gone!"

Value for Money

Gethin Griffiths was a farmer who lived near St Davids. Business was going quite well, and he wanted to buy a cow from his neighbour Dilwyn. However, on enquiring as to the price he was shocked to learn that Dilwyn wanted £50 for it. "Duw Duw, Dilwyn bach," he protested, "here am I, a good neighbour of yours all these years, and you want to charge me fifty quid for that old cow?" "Well," replied Dilwyn, "seein' as how you and me are good old friends, I'll give you 20 per cent discount."

Now Farmer Griffiths was not too good at the mathematics, so he said: "A reasonable offer, Dilwyn, but I'll need a couple of days to think about it."
Next day he was in St David's to do a spot of shopping. He was walking across the square pondering deeply about percentages and discounts when he saw the local school-mistress coming towards him. Suddenly he had a bright idea, and beckoned the good lady towards him. "Now tell me, Miss Llewellyn," he said, "if I was to offer you £50, less 20 per cent discount, what would you take off?"

Miss Llewellyn thought for a moment and said: "Everything, except my ear-rings."

Posh Words for Posh People

In the old days the residents of the top end of Milford town looked down on the people of The Rath with some amusement, for they were a well-heeled bunch who included many newcomers from "up the line". When they spoke they sounded not at all like normal Pembrokeshire people, and some of their words

and phrases were the cause of much local hilarity. One day the school-master in the local primary school was conducting a general knowledge quiz in one of the younger classes. "Now then, children," he said, "what is sex?"

"Please sir, I knows the answer!" shouted young Bert. "Sex is what them posh people on The Rath has their coal delivered in."

Still Under Guarantee

One spring Davy Evans from Newport bought a beautiful new watch from Munts the Jewellers in Haverfordwest, complete with a twelve month guarantee. Shortly before Christmas he called in at the shop again with the watch in his hand.

"Good day to you, Mr Munt bach," he said. "I has come to get my new watch fixed with you, being that I has a guarantee."

Mr Munt looked at the watch and commented that it was in a terrible state. He asked what had happened to it.

"Well now," said Davy. "It stopped workin' about six months ago, on account that it fell into the pig trough when I were feedin' the pig."

"Fair enough," said Mr Munt. "But why didn't you bring it in for repair at once?"

"Don't be daft, Mr Munt bach," replied Davy. "How could I? We only killed the pig yesterday."

Life is Tough

Young William came in with tears streaming down his face, with a bleeding nose and a black eye. After calming him down, his mother reproached him and asked him if he had been fighting again. "Yes, mam," he replied.

"And didn't you promise me that when you wanted to hit anyone you would try to control your temper by standing still and counting to a hundred?"

"So I did, Mam," wailed William. "And look what Jacky Jones did to me while I was counting."

Them What Knows

Bella and Betty were waiting in the hairdressers in Newport, reading some magazines to while away the minutes. "Well well," said Bella. "Fancy that. It says here that if you walks about in the rain without a hat or umbrella, your wrinkles will disappear. Them what knows says your complexion will look younger and younger."

"Huh!" said Betty. "Very exciting indeed. Best of luck to you, bach. There's nice it will be when they looks in your coffin after you have died of pneumonia, and says there's young and beautiful you looks."

Conversation in Narberth

Two ladies met at the check-out in the local supermarket. "Hello Mary," said one to the other. "How are you today? Terrible slugs we are having. Nice to see Mrs James up the road is out of hospital. Isn't the price of cat food something shockin' these days? Bad job about poor Mr Williams Main Street. And whatever happened to the Jones family from up the road? Haven't seen nothin' of them these ten years or more."

Ignoring the preamble, her friend Mary replied: "Oh, Billy turned out fine. He became an artist, so I hears. And Cathy became an actor, doin' plays at the Torch. Then William was a musician, so I gather, doin' records and the like. But Bert was the black sheep of the family. Never amounted to much, poor lad. It took all he could earn to support the other three."

Taking Her Time

The local minister was making a pastoral visit to a home in Amroth. There was a small baby in the house, and after a few minutes of conversation the mother went off to feed her, leaving the minister in the company of six-year-old Jacob.

"Tell me, Jacob," said the minister, "has your little sister started to talk yet?"

"Huh!" said Jacob in a disgusted tone of voice. "Not likely! She don't have to."

"What do you mean? Surely she will be starting to say little things quite soon."

"Aint no need," continued Jacob. "All she has to do is to yell like mad, and then she gets absolutely everythin' in this house that's worth havin'."

Sparkling Conversation in Croesgoch

Geraint, Gomer and Goronwy were three local farmers who used to meet up regularly, every Friday night, in the Artramont Arms for a few jars of ale. They were renowned for their sparkling conversation, which would sometimes take up the whole evening. The following conversation was overheard one evening over the course of about one hour:

Geraint: "Best glass of beer I never tasted no better."

Gomer: "So did I neither."

Goronwy: "Neither did I too."

The View from Foelcwmcerwyn

A group of intrepid English ramblers had spent a hard day hiking along the summit ridge of Mynydd Presely and at last, around sunset, they approached Presely Top or Foelcwmcerwyn. There they encountered an old shepherd, lying on his back and watching the world go by. "Good evening!" said one of the visitors. "What a lovely day it's been. And what a view! I suppose you can see for miles and miles in all directions from here?"

"Oh yes indeed," replied the old man, still lying on his back. "On a clear day you can see as far as Narberth that way, and Llangrannog that way, and Croesgoch that way, and Marloes that way."

"Good gracious, " said another of the tourists, nudging his friends and giving them a wink. "And I suppose that when it is exceptionally clear you can see as far as London?" "Oh no problem at all, at all. Much further than London, indeed."

Now the tourists were beginning to enjoy themselves. "And probably after rain you can see as far as New York out there to the west?" "Much further than New York, indeed. Most wonderful views we have here, to be sure."

Then, as the tourists were wondering about the next stage of their little joke, the old shepherd gave a good stretch and a yawn, got up, and ambled down the track towards Rosebush. He turned round and said: "If ye don't believe me, just ye sit down by here for a couple of hours, and if the clouds will just clear a bit ye'll be able to see all the way to the moon!"

Doing Well

A small boy from Broad Haven was writing a letter to his grandfather who lived in London. At the end of it he wrote the following:

"PS. The puppies that our dog had three weeks ago are coming on fine. My mam says it is because of the fresh sea air. They are growing every day. In fact having thought about it I would say that they are even growing twice a day."

Well Qualified

Dillwyn Thomas from Amroth had a few problems finding a job, and at last he decided to join the Army. He though the Welch Regiment would do nicely. He had to turn up at the Army recruiting office in Swansea for an interview, and got through the simple questions well enough. Then the recruiting officer asked him if he had any special qualifications for an Army career.

"Well now," said Dillwyn, "my Mam comes from Laugharne, and she says that Dylan Thomas is my father. On me Mam's side we are related to Lloyd George, and Phil Bennett is me uncle. Neil Kinnock is me Dad's cousin, and me Auntie Flo is the second cousin of Shirley Bassey...."

"Good God!" exclaimed the recruiting officer. "I thought we was gettin' you for fightin', not breedin'!"

A Strange Case

There were some very strange goings-on in the Army camp at Penally. Private Evans had been called up to do his National Service, but he was clearly never going to make a decent soldier. Then, about a fortnight after reporting for duty he started to behave in a most peculiar way.

"Oddest case I ever saw, Doctor," said the sergeant-major as he deposited Private Evans in the sick bay. "This lad have bin wanderin' all over the camp these last few days pickin' up bits of paper an' sayin' "This isn't it!" over an' over again. Strikes me he's off his rocker."

As if to prove the point, Private Evans rushed over to the doctor's desk and showered documents in all directions, looking at each one in turn, shouting "This isn't it!" and throwing it onto the floor. Thoroughly non-plussed, the doctor took Private Evans in and gave him a full medical examination; but he failed to find any cause for his strange condition. For the next day or two the erratic behaviour continued in the sick-bay, and at last the doctor called the sargeant-major back for a conference.

"I can't make out what's wrong with this fellow," he reported. "But whatever it is, I'm afraid he's no use at all to the Army in his present condition. He's still rushing about looking at bits of paper and shouting "This isn't it" all the time. Let somebody else try and sort him out. You'd better tell the CO. I have to recommend his immediate discharge."

Next day the sargeant-major summoned Private Evans and gave him a sheet of paper. "Here you are," he said to the young man. "You ain't no bloody good to us, that's for sure. This is your discharge paper."

Private Evans took the piece of paper, glanced at it quickly, and rushed happily from the room shouting "This is it! This is it!"

An Experienced Fighter

During the Second World War young Corporal Dafydd Rees came home on leave to Puncheston. He went over to Letterston on Saturday night for a dance in the village hall, and there he started to chat up the desirable Myfanwy. "Yes indeed," he said nonchalantly. "Got out of Dunkirk, I did, just in the nick of time. Bad business it was. Then I was lucky enough to fight with Montgomery in Libya."

Myfanwy was very impressed. "No! You didn't!" she exclaimed. "There's wonderful. Arrogant little man, so they say. And you're bigger than he is, anyway. Did you give him a good hiding?"

A Funny Name

A well-known local burglar was doing a spot of burgling in one of the more affluent suburbs of Pembroke Dock. Having affected an entry to the living room at dead of night, he prowled about, inspecting the fittings with his flashlight. Suddenly he was frightened out of his wits by a voice from the corner, which said "Jesus is watching you."

Having recovered his composure, the burglar shone his torch in the direction of the voice, and saw a parrot sitting on its perch inside a cage. "Did you say that?" he asked the parrot. "Of course I did," replied the bird. "And what's your name?" asked the burglar. "Jennifer," said the parrot.

The burglar laughed and said "Jennifer the parrot? That's really funny."

"Not half as funny as Jesus the rottweiler," said the parrot.

A Cosy Present

Mabel went into the wool shop in Fishguard, and after having a bit of a chat she explained that she wanted some wool to make a winter coat for her poodle. "How much wool do you want?" asked the shop assistant.

"I really wouldn't know," replied Mabel.

"Well, what size is your dog?"

"It's not very big and not very small, but sort of middling," said Mabel.

"That makes things a bit difficult. Why don't you bring the dog in, so that we can measure it up and work it out exactly?" suggested the assistant.

"Oh, I couldn't do that. It's supposed to be a surprise."

Value for Money

Little Ethel was being particularly unbearable, and eventually her mother could stand it no longer. "Ethel!" she shouted. "Yesterday I gave you a penny to be good, and you behaved like a little angel. Today you are being perfectly horrible. What on earth has got into you?"

"Well mam," replied the little girl, "I am just trying to show you today how well spent that penny was yesterday!"

Checking for Quality

There was an old tramp who used to frequent the Maenclochog area. One day he went into the village shop, having spotted some freshly baked buns in the window. "Mornin' missus," he said to the shop-keeper. "How much are them nice lookin' buns in the window?"

"A penny each," replied the shopkeeper. Before she could react, the old tramp grabbed a bun from the shelf and took a great bite out of it. "That's not too bad at all, missus," he said appreciatively. "I'll take a ha'penny worth if you please!"

Naturally enough, the shopkeeper had to give him the bun before she threw him out.

Just Making Sure

Two old timers met in the Post Office in Llangwm. "Hast tha heard?" said one to the other. "They've gone an' buried John Palmer yesterday."

"Get away man!" said the other. "Is a dead then?"

Adequate Proof

Some years ago a visitor to Marloes called at the Post Office to collect a registered packet that had been sent to him in advance "to await arrival." The lady at the counter was very conscientious, and had recently been warned by the Postmaster General to be very strict on security matters. So she refused to accept that the visitor was really the person for whom the packet was intended. "Have you no means of identifying yourself?" she asked. "Passport, driving license, or cheque book?"

"Nothing at all," said the visitor. Then he thought for a moment and took out a photograph from his inside pocket. "But this is a photo of myself which I took in one of those machines on Paddington Station."

The lady behind the counter looked at it carefully, and then looked the visitor in the eye. "Well, sir," she said after due deliberation. "I can definitely see the likeness. Whoever you are, you are certainly not somebody else, so here is the packet you asked for."

Crisis Management

During the First World War two Pembrokeshire soldiers were posted, after training at Fort Scoveston, to the trenches in France. One of them was Joe "Keek" Davies from Haverfordwest, and the other was his pal Wiffie Davies. Things were not going well for the British troops, and at last Keek and Wiffie found themselves isolated in a trench under constant bombardment and with no surviving colleagues anywhere in the vicinity. Suddenly they realised that about three hundred German soldiers were advancing towards them, and that they had no hope of retreat. All was lost, and the men decided that surrender was the only option.

"Quick, Wiffie," said Keek. "Have you got anything white that we can wave for the Jerries?"

"Afraid not," replied Wiffie. "The only white thing I had was my underpants, but I'm so bloody scared that they ain't white any longer!"

The Art of Child Management

Franklin Jenkins was a spoilt and precocious child who lived in a smart house at the posh end of Tenby. One day a new nurse was appointed to look after him. On their first meeting Franklin looked her over suspiciously and said, with hostility in his voice: "Huh! I suppose you'd be my new nurse?"

"Yes dear, I am," replied the girl.

"Well then," said Franklin, "I overheard my mother saying to you when you had your interview that I am one of those children who can only be managed by kindness, so you'd better start off by getting me a slice of chocolate cake and a can of coke, or else there'll be big trouble."

Ask a Stupid Question....

Once upon a time an English visitor to Stackpole Court was walking through the woodland on the estate when he came across a local peasant standing alongside a decayed tree with a crosscut saw in his hand.

"And what are you intending to do with that saw, my good man?" asked the visitor.

"I'm gwain to cut'n down, sir," replied the peasant.

"And then what are you going to do?"

"That's a hard question, sir," said the local, "but after thinkin' about it I reckons I'd better cut'n up."

Tom Eynon the Witch

Tom Eynon was feared by almost everybody. He lived at The Rock, near Lamphey, and it was well known that if you happened to get on the wrong side of him he was quite likely to "cast the evil eye" on you, leading to endless trouble. There were various tales in circulation around 1840, one of which involved a bewitching of a butter churn. But then things rebounded on Tom, much to the delight of the locals.

Tom was married twice. He treated his first wife very harshly, and never gave her sufficient money to pay for food and other household needs. The poor woman led a miserable existence, and matters were not helped by the way in which most of the locals kept well clear of her husband. When she died, Tom waited for a respectable period of time and then he married again. The locals felt sorry for the new wife, assuming that the poor woman would have just as miserable a time as her predecessor. Right in the middle of the wedding night, at a very embarrassing moment, who should appear next to the bed but the very angry ghost of Tom's first wife. "Tom! Tom!" she cried. "Give me some money, give me some money!" Tom's new wife was terrified by the apparition and fled downstairs. Tom was very angry but perhaps not very surprised, since he had frequent encounters with the spirit world. He knew how to get rid of ghosts, and drove the phantom away. However, nothing would induce his new wife to return to bed that night, and indeed she was so frightened by the experience that it took many weeks before he could coax her back to the marriage bed. This episode did no good at all for Tom's sex life, and it caused much amusement in the local community. Needless to say, after this, he treated his second wife considerably better than his first.

A Practical Man

In 1973 Mr Ivor John of Haverfordwest fell ill, and had to spend a short time in Withybush Hospital. In the next bed there was an old man who ran a little farm up in the Presely Hills. The two men spent a great deal of time chatting together, and one day the conversation turned to children and grand-children. Ivor mentioned that he had six grand-children, and not to be out-done, his neighbour laughed and proclaimed that he had no less than fifteen. Ivor was duly impressed.

"You are indeed well blessed," he said. "But don't you find it rather an expensive blessing? Fifteen birthday presents distributed through the year, and then at Christmas fifteen gifts all at the same time! How on earth do you manage?"

"Oh, I do manage," said the old farmer, very slowly. "I do sell a cow!"

The Buckingham Palace Geranium

Once upon a time, not very long ago, a certain local hero from a small Pembrokeshire town was invited to a Buckingham Palace Garden Party. (The name of the town cannot be divulged for reasons of national security, but suffice to say that it is quite a long way from almost everywhere.) Having been duly decorated by the Queen our hero and his family spent a happy time in the Buckingham Palace garden, mingling in the vast crowd, drinking tea and enjoying a cucumber sandwich or two. Suddenly his attention was attracted in the flower borders by a most unusual geranium with abundant smallish blossoms of a delightful orange-red colour. He was overcome with the desire to own just a little of the wonderful geranium, and after sidling up to it and making sure that all the other guests were looking the other way he snipped off a little piece with his fingers and popped it into his pocket.

When the Garden Party was over he managed to escape without being searched, and on reaching his car he wrapped the cutting in a damp piece of newspaper for safekeeping. After the long drive home he dipped it into a little rooting hormone powder and put it in a pot to see if it would survive. And sure enough, the geranium created roots, and grew and grew into a thing of beauty. Before long the fame of "The Buckingham Palace Geranium" had spread far and wide throughout the town, and one person, and then another, and another, were presented with cuttings which they propagated and nurtured. Their geraniums bloomed beautifully, and so they presented yet more cuttings to yet more neighbours.......

And so it is that today, when you go into almost any house in this little town, and when you see a beautiful geranium in a place of honour in the front room, you must, according to tradition, say "What a beautiful geranium! What sort is it?" And, naturally enough, back will come the reply "Oh, THAT is the Buckingham Palace geranium."

The Fools of Strumble Head

Once upon a time there were some foolish fellows who lived at Llanwnwr, near Strumble Head. They bought a round cheese at Fishguard Fair. Just as they reached home, the fool who was carrying the cheese dropped it, and it rolled downhill along the lane leading to the sea. They chased after it, not too fast, in case they should overtake it. One of the fools jumped over the hedge and ran on the other side, as one does when one is driving cattle. Soon the cheese came to the cliff edge and rolled straight over, crashing down into the sea far below. The fools agreed that they could get at it by hanging over the edge of the cliff, each one taking hold of the ankles of the one above. When all was ready, with all three dangling in space, the top fool said "Let me get a better grip. I must spit on my hands." And down they all went after the cheese, never to be seen again.

Getting It Over With

An old farmer from up in the hills near Tufton had to go to Withybush Hospital for an operation. As soon as he arrived he was undressed by two young nurses and given a good bath.

As he left the bathroom he turned to one of the nurses and said: "Well, bach, there's glad I am that that's over. It wasn't so bad after all. To tell you the truth I've been dreading that operation these five years or more."

Living Together

Two old brothers lived together in a little farmhouse near Mynachlogddu. One of them met a friend at Crymych mart, and was clearly in a bad mood. On being asked what was the matter, he replied: "That bloody brother of mine makes life unbearable at times, he does. He keeps all them dogs and cats in the bedroom, and sheep in the kitchen and goats in the dinin' room. It smells terrible, and they do say that such things is unhealthy too."

"Well, why don't you open the windows?" asked the friend.

"What?" exclaimed the old brother. "And let all my pigeons escape?"

Lust for Power

Dai Jones of Pembroke Dock was greatly involved in local politics, like a lot of other Joneses in Pembrokeshire. One day he was elected onto the local council, and his newly acquired status went to his head. He announced to his wife, and to all his friends, that henceforth he wished to be referred to as "Councillor Jones." Then he went out for a night on the town in order to celebrate his great victory.

Coming back late from the pub, he made a great commotion trying to unlock the front door in order to get into the house. "Is that you, Dai?" shouted his wife from the top of the stairs.

"Get it right, woman!" replied Dai. "This is Councillor Jones."

"Well, come on up quick then," said the wife. "We've only got a few minutes before Dai gets back from the pub."

Careful Policing

A young policeman from Fishguard was drafted up to London to help with the Coronation. Everything in the big city was new to him. He was given orders to stand outside Westminster Abbey and to take charge of a certain door. He was told that nobody but the highest dignitaries were to be allowed in that way. As he stood to attention a dignified Minister of the Crown approached, and was ordered by the young policeman to stand back. "I am told, sir, that I cannot let you in by this door."

"But," said the irritated gentleman, "I am a Cabinet Minister."

"I don't care even if you are a bloody Baptist minister, sir. I have got me orders, and cannot let you in."

Abraham's Fire

Abraham Arabia was a successful Jewish businessman who had a thriving draper's shop in the main street of a Pembrokeshire town. One day he was in Haverfordwest on business, and Charlie James the Cobbler met him on the street. "Good day, Abraham," said Charlie. "I was very sorry to hear the sad news."

"What sad news?" asked Abraham.

"About your shop going on fire last Tuesday. Isaac Evans told me."

"Husht, you fool!" exclaimed Abraham. "Don't talk so loud, somebody will hear you. It is **next** Tuesday."

Danger For The King

In the early part of this century there were two rival butchers on opposite sides of the Main Street in Pembroke. Both of them made excellent sausages, and they competed vigorously for the custom of the townspeople. One day a sign appeared over the shop-front of Butcher Morgan, with the legend: "We sell sausages to the gentry and nobility of the county."

The next day, over the shop-front of Butcher Edwards across the way, appeared the sign: "We sell sausages to the gentry and nobility of the whole kingdom."

Not to be out-done, Butcher Morgan responded with a sign which he considered to be the end of the affair: "We sell sausages to the king."

Next day there appeared over the door of Butcher Edwards' shop the simple legend: "God Save the King."

Getting Stronger by the Day

A visitor to Fishguard heard that old Sid Roberts had recently celebrated his hundredth birthday. Never having met a centenarian before, he paid a visit in order to give his respects. In the course of the conversation the visitor congratulated Sid on his hail and hearty appearance, and added as a joke "But I presume you do not expect to see out another hundred years?" The old man thought for a while.

"Well now, you never can tell," he replied. "For sure I'm a good deal stronger now than when I started with the first hundred."

Tenby Rabbit Pie

Before the scourge of myxomatosis afflicted Pembrokeshire, a certain restaurant in Tenby was famous for its rabbit pie. But then, with the coming of the disease, the proprietor, Joseph Jones, found it increasingly difficult to get rabbit supplies. The customers, some of whom came from as far away as Penally just for the rabbit pie, noticed a distinct decline in the taste and texture of the meat.

Eventually the rumour went around that the restaurant was using horse-meat in the pie, and one day some of the customers confronted the proprietor.

"Joseph", said one, "your rabbit pie is not what it used to be. Now then, give us a straight answer to this question: are you using horse-meat in the pie mixture?"

"Yes, indeed," said the boss. "I have nothing to hide. Rabbits are not easy to find these days, and I find that a bit of horse-flesh adds greatly to the subtle flavour of the pie."

"So how much horse-meat do you use?"

"Half and half."

"You mean fifty-fifty?"

"Of course," replied Joseph.

"Don't I make myself clear? One horse to one rabbit."

Cowardice is Alive and Well

Tommy Twopence and Billy Bovver were involved in an acrimonious dispute, the origins of which were largely forgotten. The dispute was much discussed in the pubs of Pembroke. One day Billy insulted Tommy to his face, and the latter's friends were outraged when their man simply turned away as if he had heard nothing. "Tommy," said one of them, "that Billy Bovver is gettin' too big for his boots. You has to do somethin' about it, boy."

"But look at the size of him, "replied Tommy. "The man's a giant, an' with a nasty temper, too."

"Very well," said the disgusted friend, "that's up to you. But all the lads down in the club'll say you're nothin' but a yellow-bellied coward."

Tommy thought for a moment. "Well, I dunno'," he responded with the air of a saint. "At any rate, I'd rather have 'em sayin' that than have 'em lookin' into a long box the day after tomorrow an' exclaimin': How natural Tommy looks!"

Make Him Walk

Young Johnny had passed his Eleven Plus exam, and had been given a place in Haverfordwest Grammar School. A few days after he started school, a smart salesman knocked on the door of his house. His father answered the door.

"Good day, sir!" said the salesman. "I must congratulate your son on obtaining a place in the Grammar School, a most excellent seat of learning. You must be the proud father. In order to help your son to make rapid progress through his academic career, have you ever thought of getting him an encyclopaedia?"

"Rubbish," said Johnny's dad. "Walking to school was good enough for me when I was his age, and he can do the same!"

Recipe For Long Life

Caleb and Jimmy were making their unsteady way home from the funeral of a friend. They got to talking about the uncertainty of life, and Caleb suddenly came over all philosophical. "For sure," he said, "I'd give all I've got, Jimmy bach, if I knew the place where I was goin' to die."

"Don't be daft, man. What good would that do ye?"

"Well, I'd go a tidy step never to go near the place, that's for sure."

Elected To High Office

One morning Gwynfor Masonry did not arrive at work in Crymych until almost lunch-time. When he turned up his boss summoned him to the building site office and gave him a good dressing-down. "Very sorry I am, boss," said Gwynfor, "but I had a big meeting last night with the lodge."

"Well," said the boss, "that's no reason for you to be late this morning."

"But I had a great deal to do this morning after being elected to high office."

"And what office was that?"

"The brethren elected me Grand Exalted High Ruler of the Universe."

"Good gracious! That sounds very impressive for a man as young as yourself."

"Greatly honoured I am, to be sure, boss. But to be honest, Grand Exalted Ruler of the Universe is the lowest office in the Crymych Lodge, and this mornin' I had to go back to the hall to pick up the cold chips off the floor, mend the chairs, wipe the beer off the walls, and wash the glasses."

Much The Same

In the bad old days life was tough up in the Presely Hills, and the smallholders enjoyed few luxuries in life. Will met Twm in the "Drover's Arms" in Puncheston.

"Come and have a bite to eat with me tonight," he said. "Not much - just boiled beef, spuds and carrots."

"Most generous of you, Will," replied Twm. "Happy to accept, I am. It's a funny thing, but I was goin' to have exactly the same for supper meself, barrin' the beef and the carrots."

Small Accident in Saundersfoot

Morgan Liquid Refreshment lived in Saundersfoot, and was so named because of his habit of consuming too much, too often. One day an Englishman moved to the village, and discovered that he and Morgan shared a taste for fine Scotch whisky. He invited Morgan round for a glass or two, and when it was time for Morgan to go the Englishman said: "Here, Morgan, there is a spot of the Scotch left in the bottle. You have it with my compliments; I'll put it here in your coat pocket, so that you can enjoy another little drink when you get home."

Morgan was almost moved to tears by this gesture. He thanked the kind Englishman, put on his coat and took his leave.

Now it happened that there was a hard frost that night. On the way home Morgan, somewhat unsteady on his feet, slipped on the pavement and fell to the ground with an almighty crash. He was knocked out for a minute or two; and when he came to he could feel something liquid running down his leg. "Good Heavens!" he exclaimed. "I hope to God it's blood."

Tough Times on the Hustings

At a parliamentary election campaign meeting on the Salutation Square in Haverfordwest, the candidate was having a hard time trying to convince the voters of his worth. As he spoke it became increasingly clear to him that the meeting was packed with supporters of his rival, the sitting MP. At last he stopped his speech and exclaimed indignantly to the chairman. "Mr Chairman, I have been on my feet for nearly ten minutes, but there is so much noise and interruption that I can hardly hear myself speak."

"Cheer up, guv'nor, "came a voice from the back of the crowd. "Tha ain't missin' much."

At last the chairman restored order and the candidate continued. "Fellow citizens," he said. "I am the man you need to represent this constituency in the mother of Parliaments. I have been to the North-West Frontier and fought hand-to-hand with the wild men of the mountains. I have fought the Zulus under the raging sun of Africa. Often I have had no bed but the battlefield and no canopy but the sky. I have marched the frozen wastes of Canada until every step was an agony. For King and country I have sailed the seven seas, soaked by mountainous waves....."

At last the voice from the back of the crowed intervened again. "After all that, guv'nor," it said, "I should say tha's done quite enough for thy country. For God's sake go home an' have a rest. I reckons we'd all better vote for th' other chap -- a don't do much, but at least a's not worn out."

Buying Some Land

Back in the bad old days many English people were attracted to Pembrokeshire by the low price of land. One smart operator from London liked the look of a farm not far from Wiston, which was on the market. He thought he might be able to acquire it for a song. He went to visit the farmer, who turned out to be an old man living in squalid conditions. "Good day to you, sir," said the Londoner. "I am interested in buying some of your land."

"How much?" asked the farmer.

"About a thousand pounds' worth," said the visitor, waving his arm out over the rolling countryside.

"Come back tomorrow then," said the old man evenly. "And don't forget your wheelbarrow."

All it Needs

John Thomas the Auctioneer was selling some building plots on a new housing estate in Haverfordwest. Things were a bit slow, and he was finding it difficult to dispose of the plots at anywhere near the prices expected. So like a good auctioneer he started to work himself up to a poetic state. With a great flourish he waved his arms over the still-derelict territory before him and said: "Ladies and gentlemen, imagine this place in ten years time! Dry and dusty it may be at this moment, but will spring into life, with houses and lawns and flowers and shrubs and happy laughing children! Take my word for it, all it needs to become the garden of the world is good people and water..."

"Yes indeed," came a voice from the crowd. "That's all Hell needs, too. An' that's why most folks tries to go to the other place, where it's a bit wetter an' where one won't keep on bumpin' into the mother-in-law."

Willy's Secret System

Willy Wilkins of Marloes won the Pembrokeshire Lottery, and after being presented with his cheque for £2000 he threw a great party in the village for all his friends and relatives. Somebody asked him how he had come to win.

"Well boys," said Willy. "I has this infallible system for winnin' lotteries. I goes to sleep at night an' dreams of a number. Then I goes to sleep the next night an' dreams of another number. Then I multiplies the one by the other, and I knows I'll be in the big money."

"Amazing!" said cousin Arnold. "An' what was your winnin' ticket number?"

"Forty-two," said Willy. "First night I dreamt of a number seven, and the second night I dreamt of a number seven. So I thought to meself, seven multiplied by seven makes forty-two, an' that's how I knew the cheque was on its way even before the draw was drew."

Too Good to Miss

Sam Storey was an old tramp who originated in Southern Ireland. One day he came over to Pembrokeshire on the ferry from Rosslare, and never went away again. Generally he was referred to in the north of the county as "Saymold Storey" for reasons which should be obvious. Normally he would be seen but once a year on the streets of St David's, but this year was an exception. He knocked on a door of a fine house on Cross Square, to be confronted by the wife of the local doctor. Immediately he asked if she might be able to spare a sandwich for a poor lonely man who had fallen on hard times.

"If I am not very much mistaken, " the lady of the house replied angrily, "you are the very same dirty, worthless vagabond that knocked on my door two weeks ago, begging for food."

"Indeed I am, missus," replied Sam, removing his greasy trilby hat with a flourish and bowing low. "My name is Samuel Storey. It is a pleasure to visit you again. I had to call to tell you, madam, that the corned beef sandwich I had with you on my last call was the most tasty and subtle I ever ate. The meat was perfection itself, and the mustard set it off a treat. And as for the bread -- it was like manna from heaven, delivered fresh from the Pearly Gates. Now I must continue on me way, bein' that I has urgent matters to attend to down in Solva. But since I am here, I might as well ask. There would not be a chance, would there madam, that there might still be a slice left in the bottom of the can?"

A Wise Precaution

Toby Thomas from Solva went to sea, like many others from his village. What's more, he could write, and the officer on board his first ship was greatly impressed when, in signing a document, Toby signed the first part of his name with his left hand and the second part with his right. "Very impressive," said the officer. "We don't get many ambidextrous people on the crew of this ship."

Toby did not know many long words, but he assumed this was some sort of a compliment. "No problem, sire," he replied. "When I was a boy me father - God rest his soul, for he drowned in the Bay of Biscay - always said to me: Toby, you just learn to cut your finger-nails with your left hand, for some day you might lose your right."

Unrequited Love

They do say that in the matter of love, the boys of Spittal are a bit backward at coming forward. Young Danny was courting a sweet girl called Mavis, and when he acquired a second-hand Morris Minor he invited her for a drive around the countryside. Mavis leapt at the chance, for she was very much in love with Danny.

After being driven around Pembrokeshire for a couple of hours with no sign of a breakdown, and with Danny clearly obsessed with his new car, Mavis decided to take the initiative. "Danny," she said, "I feel miserable."

"That's very bad," said Danny. "What's the trouble?"

"Nobody loves me, and my hands are cold."

"Dammo, you should not speak like that, Mavis," said Danny reprovingly, at 20 mph and with his eyes on the road, "God loves you, your mother loves you, and you can always sit on your hands."

Chapter Five

RELIGION IS GOOD FOR YOU

The Very Wicked Monks

In the bad old days there were two very wicked monks, Brother Aeron and Brother Bryn, who belonged to the monastery on Caldey Island. Brother Aeron went to the Abbot, whose name was Pyro, to confess his sins. "Father, I have sinned," he said. "Woe is me, for I have broken my vows of celibacy with a married woman."

"With a married woman!" exclaimed Abbot Pyro. "Carnal knowledge is a mortal sin, my son. Now, you must tell me the name of the evil female with whom you have slept."

"I cannot tell you that, Father. It would not be honourable."

"Aeron, my son, let me be the judge of that. Now who was it? Was it by any chance Llinos the wife of Glyn the Weaver of Penally?"

"No, no, Father, it was not her, but more than that I cannot say.

"My son, your wickedness is indeed terrible. Do you realise that your sin is confounded by your hiding of the truth? Now tell me -- was it Eluned the wife of Merfyn the Miller?"

"Father, forgive me, but it was not her. I cannot reveal to any man who it was."

At last the Abbot tired of his interrogation and said: "Aeron, you have done a dastardly deed. If you will not tell me who has led you astray, away with you and do your penance! Say ten Hail Marys and empty the latrines for a fortnight."

Outside the confessional Aeron met his friend Brother Bryn. "How was it?" whispered Bryn. "What did you get?"

"It went fine," replied Aeron under his breath. "Ten Hail Marys, toilet duty, and a couple of very good leads."

A Hard Choice

It was a dark winter's evening, and sheets of rain were sweeping across the Pembrokeshire landscape. Rev Hywel Huws was in inspired mood as he launched into his sermon in the pulpit of Bethesda Chapel in Narberth. He took as his text the parable of the five wise and five foolish virgins. At great length, and with not a little oratory, he explained the meaning of the parable and came to the matter of moral choices. Building to a mighty climax, he confronted his nodding congregation with the final challenge. "Now then, my friends," he bellowed, "you have to face this dilemma fair and square. Where would you rather be? Where indeed? With the wise virgins in the light .... or with the foolish virgins in the dark?" Afterwards he noticed that all the men in the congregation went home with dreamy smiles on their faces, and wondered what had got into them.

Jogging the Memory

Rev Idwal Jenkins was the minister of Hill Park Baptist Chapel in Haverfordwest. One day he complained to Billy Evans, one of the chapel deacons, that his bicycle was missing. "I don't like to point an accusing finger," he said, "but I have a feeling that young Jimmy from Coronation Avenue has pinched it. Do you think I should go and look for it?"

"No no," replied Billy. "That would be very embarrassing. The simplest way to catch the culprit is to preach a sermon on the Ten Commandments next Sunday. When you get to "Thou shalt not steal", look very carefully at the congregation, and sure as eggs you'll spot the guilty person." The minister congratulated Billy on his brilliant idea, and decided to put the plan into effect.

On Sunday morning Rev Jenkins started his sermon in fine style, but as it went on he quite lost the thread of what he was saying and ended in a complete muddle. Afterwards Billy commiserated with him in the chapel vestry. "What on earth went wrong, reverend?" he asked. "Well, Billy," replied the minister, "everything was going quite well until I got to "Thou shalt not commit adultery", and then I remembered where I left my bicycle."

A Proper Baptist

A man from Haverfordwest was travelling on an ocean voyage, and was looking forward to arriving back at Fishguard Harbour. However, not far from home a mighty storm blew up and he was shipwrecked on Grassholm Island. He was the only survivor, but huge piles of flotsam and jetsam from the wrecked ship were washed onto the rocks. The storm continued for several weeks, but at last he was spotted by the crew of a passing ship. A rescue party was put ashore on the

island, and the men were amazed to see that it was covered with fine buildings made from stout timbers, canvas and ships fittings.

The man from Harfat took them on a guided tour, proudly pointing out to them his house, his workshop, his electricity generator, a pub and two Baptist chapels. "Ah, the pub looks very cosy," said the first mate. "I sees that you have got your priorities right." The shipwrecked traveller looked shocked. "Not at all," he replied. "I built this little pub so as to help me to resist temptation." The first mate was somewhat taken aback by this, but then he asked: "The two chapels then. Why have you gone to all the trouble to build two Baptist chapels, for goodness sake?"

"Don't be daft, man," said the man from Harfat. "One has to keep up appearances. That one over by there is the one I goes to, and this one over by here is the one I stays away from."

Another Soul Saved

Arthur Amen was a good Christian gentleman who had come over all religious during an evangelical campaign in Wesley Chapel in Haverfordwest. One day he was out for a walk on the cliffs near Dale when he lost his footing and fell over the edge. He managed to grab hold of a gorse bush halfway down the cliff, and dangled there above a sheer drop.

A passing tourist threw a rope down to him and offered to pull him up, but Arthur shouted: "No thanks. The great preacher told me that I am saved, so God will rescue me."

Then a passing boatman shouted to Arthur from below, and told him to jump into the water and be saved. "No thank you," said Arthur. "God will rescue me." A few minutes later the RAF Brawdy helicopter passed by, and the winch-man let down a rope ladder for Arthur to clamber up. Again he said: "No thanks. God will rescue me."

Finally a submarine popped up in the sea below the cliff, and an officer shouted through a loud-hailer for Arthur to jump. "No thanks," shouted Arthur. "I'm all right. My Lord will save me."

A few minutes later Arthur ran out of energy, let go of the gorse bush, fell into the sea and was drowned. As he stood before the Pearly Gates God came out to meet him. "Oh God," said Arthur. "Why didn't you save me in my hour of need?"

"Look, my child," replied God. "I sent you a rope, a boat, a helicopter and a submarine. What more did you expect me to do?"

Heaven is Close at Hand

Two small children from Tenby were speculating on theological matters. Turning to his sister Annie, young Gareth said: "I wonder where God lives." Annie replied: "Huh! That's easy. I knows exactly where God lives. He lives in the bathroom."

"Rubbish," said Gareth. "The bathroom is far too small. And who told you that anyway?"

"Well", insisted Annie, "I worked it out, because every morning when Daddy goes to the bathroom he prowls back and forth in front of the door in a filthy mood shouting: God, are you still in there?"

Never on a Sunday

The corner sweet shop in Fishguard was open on a Sunday morning, so Mr Smythe, who was on holiday in the town, called in to buy a bar of chocolate. When he asked for his Mars bar, the old lady behind the counter replied: "Oh, very sorry I am, sir. But I can't sell you a bar of chocolate."

"Why on earth not?" asked Mr Smythe. "You have just sold some peppermints to the little girl who has just gone out."

"Ah, but that's a different thing. I sells peppermints on a Sunday because they takes them to church to eat, and they do say it helps them to keep awake in the sermon so as to become good Christian people. They are **Sabbath** sweets. But as for chocolates, that is a different matter. If you wants a bar of chocolate you must come on a week-day, since bars of chocolate counts as being **secular** sweets."

Joffre Goes to Rome

Joffre Swales is well known all over Pembrokeshire and further afield for his stirling work in encouraging young musicians. Once upon a time he went to Rome with his Brass Band, and after performing heroically in St Peter's Square Joffre and the youngsters were treated to tea in the Vatican. The Pope invited Joffre into his chambers for a little chat, but then a Cardinal came in and reminded the Pope that it was time to go out and wave from the balcony to the assembled faithful below. "Come out onto the balcony with me," said the Pope to Joffre. "The view is quite wonderful." So Joffre followed the Holy Father out as he delivered his daily blessing on half a million people in the square below.

Just then a couple of tourists passed by. They happened to be from Honey Harfat, and they were on a package deal holiday to Italy. One said to the other: "Ooh, look, there's two people up there on that balcony wavin' to the crowd. I wonder who they are?"

"One of them is Joffre Swales wavin' to his fans," said his friend. "God knows who the other one in the funny outfit is. Maybe it's his Italian agent."

By Way of Explanation

Sid Stephens, the chapel steward of the little Methodist Chapel in Merlin's Bridge, was pressed into service at very short notice when the appointed preacher for the morning failed to turn up. He got through a few hymns, bible readings and prayers all right, and then got to the sermon. After a short supplication for heavenly guidance, he started off, not knowing quite where his train of thought would lead him.

"Now then, dear brothers and sisters," he said. "I has it in my mind to talk about the miracle of the water bein' turned into wine. A most wonderful phenomeno it was, praise be to the Lord."

Before he could continue, a voice piped up from the back row, "Please Sid, what is a phenomeno?"

"I am glad you asked me that, Brother Thomas," he replied. "Tis a fine new word I came across just th'other day. Not bein' a Doctor of Philosophics, I'll explain it to thee as simple as I can. If, for example, tha sees a cow producin' a gallon of milk, that is not a phenomeno. If tha sees a blackbird sittin' on top of a pine tree singin' his heart out, that is not a phenomeno. If tha sees a sewin swimmin' up the river under the New Bridge, that is not a phenomeno. However, me dear brothers and sisters, if tha sees a milkin' cow swimmin' up the river under the New Bridge an' singin' a beautiful melody at the same time, then **that** is surely a phenomeno."

Helping the Work of God

Young Mary Jane was six years old, and it was her first Sunday in Wesley methodist Church in Haverfordwest. Before the service she was given a penny by her mother and told to put it into the collection bag when it came round.

After the service the girl turned excitedly to her mother and said: "Mam! When the lucky bag came round I put in my penny and got out a sixpenny piece! What did you get?"

Keeping the Sabbath

Brynmor lived in Maenclochog. One fine day he was hammering away at the bottom of his wheelbarrow in the garden when his wife came to the kitchen door.

"Brynmor!" she exclaimed. "There's a terrible racket you are making, and on the Sabbath too! What will the neighbours say?"

"I couldn't care less about the neighbours, Blodwen bach," replied Brynmor. "But I has to get me barra fixed for cleanin' out the chicken shed."

"But husband bach, it's very wrong to work on the Sabbath," said Blodwen, full of righteous indignation. "It's screws you should be using."

The Price of Innocence

In Wolfscastle School the teacher was giving a Religious Instruction lesson, and she asked Johnny who had knocked down the Walls of Jericho. "Honest, miss," replied Johnny, "it wasn't me."

The teacher was most concerned at Johnny's lack of religious knowledge, and next time she met his mother in the street she said: "I'm very worried about young Johnny. When I asked him who had knocked down the Walls of Jericho he simply said that it wasn't him. He should know better." Immediately Johnny's Mam became very irate, and said: "Don't you dare accuse my Johnny. If he said he didn't knock the Walls of Jericho down, then he didn't do it."

Now the teacher was even more concerned, and some days later she called in to see Johnny's father. She told him about the episode, and immediately he took out his wallet. "Now then, Mrs Jones bach," he said. "We don't want any trouble at the school. Just tell me how much that wall cost, and we'll put things right."

A Delicate Question

Young Joshua Williams and his pretty wife Megan were faithful members of Bethesda Chapel in Haverfordwest before their marriage, but after the happy day their attendance at Sunday service fell off somewhat. The Minister, Rev Hopcyn Hopkins, called round to see if there was something wrong. "Well, reverend," said Joshua, "we have a difficult and delicate question of religion which Megan and I can't decide for ourselves. What we want to know is whether it is allright for us to have sex after chapel on Sunday mornings."

"Now that is a very difficult question," replied the minister. "I shall have to consult with the deacons about it." He went away, and Joshua and Megan heard nothing more until a fortnight had passed. Then Rev Hopkins called round again, and was welcomed into the house. "We are very glad to see you," said Megan. "So what decision have you come to?"

"We had a very lovely meeting about it," replied the minister. "The discussion went on for five hours, and we examined the matter from many different angles."

"Yes, but what did you decide?"

"Mr Willy Williams spoke with great eloquence, and left me greatly moved," said the minister.

"Yes, yes, but what was your theological decision?"

"And Mr Tommy Thomas gave us a most learned discourse quoting many wonderful thoughts from the scriptures."

"But what conclusion did you reach, Mr Hopkins?"

"Oh, at the end of it all we decided it is all right, provided you don't enjoy it."

The Right Jones

Dai Jones went to Heaven a few years before his wife; and when she finally arrived she thought she would try and meet up with him again. So she went to St Peter and asked if there was a Mr Jones on his little list of residents. "Madam," replied the Saint, "we have got millions of Joneses here. What is his first name?" Mrs Jones told him, and he said: "Oh dear. That's not good enough. We have thousands of Dai Joneses too. Where did he live?" "In Pembrokeshire", said the good wife. "Still not good enough," said St Peter. "We have hundreds of Dai Joneses from Pembrokeshire. Can't you think of anything else that will help us to check our records?"

After giving it a lot of thought, Mrs Jones said: "Well, he did say as he lay on his death-bed that if I was to sleep with any other man after he was dead and gone, he would turn in his grave."

"Oh, that makes all the difference," said St Peter. "I know exactly who you are talking about. Up here we call him Revolving Jones."

A Gift for God

The Salvation Army were involved in a mission in Pembroke Dock, and at one of their meetings an old tramp, who hailed from Cardigan, decided to go along in order to enjoy the warmth and the music. He had a splendid time, and got a bowl of steaming soup into the bargain. At the end of the meeting a pretty young lady in Salvation Army uniform went round with a bowl, asking all those present whether they would give "sixpence to God."

When she came up to the old tramp he said to her "Tell me, young lady, how old are you?" "Well," replied the girl, "that's a very personal question, but I'll tell you anyway. I am twenty years old."

"Is that so?" replied the Cardi. "There's nice, and very pretty you are too. But I'll tell you what. I'm seventy-five, and I've only got threepence in me pocket. I'll no doubt be seein' the Almighty afore you do, so I'll give him the threepence meself."

Personal Religion

Visitors to Pembrokeshire are often confused by the multiplicity of churches, chapels and religious denominations which confront them on all sides. The tendency towards schism continued until quite recent times.

Gomer Griffiths and his wife Nansi, together with a few friends, split off from their local Baptist Chapel because they could no longer accept its doctrines. (At least, that was their story. The real reason was that Mrs Jones Penbanc forgot to put Nansi down on the rota for flower arranging.) Some months later the minister met Gomer and asked him whether he and the others were worshipping together.

"Well, not exactly," replied Gomer. "We have discovered certain differences between us, so Nansi and me have withdrawn from Communion with them."

"That is very unfortunate," said the minister. ""So I suppose you and your wife carry on your devotions together at home?"

"Well, not exactly," said Gomer. "We found that our views on certain doctrines were not in harmony, so there has been a division between us. You see, I have discovered that I am by inclination a United English Reformed Presbyterian. She, on the other hand, is instinctively a Traditional Welsh Wesleyan Baptist. She therefore worships in the kitchen, and I take the living room."

By Way of Explanation

Billy Evans of Hook was a retired coal-miner who became a Methodist lay preacher. One Sunday morning he was down to take the service in Llangwm Methodist Chapel. He took as the text for his sermon some words from Chapter 60 of the Book of Isaiah: "For behold the darkness shall cover the earth and gross darkness the people."

"Brothers and sisters," said Billy. "I knows from my time workin' the two-foot seam in Hook Colliery what darkness is all about. All us miners knows what it's like when the lamp goes out. Isn't that right, boys? So that's darkness for you. But what about this 'ere gross darkness that Brother Isaiah is talkin' about? Well, when I was at school Miss Beynon taught us that a gross is one hundred and forty four. Therefore, brothers and sisters, you will understand accordingly that gross darkness is 144 times darker than the darkness what is in the two-foot seam."

A True Conversion

Wally Williams lived in the Gwaun Valley and was a faithful member of Jabez Baptist Chapel. However, both he and his wife Llinos were frequently reprimanded by the members of the congregation for their heavy drinking. Indeed, it had been observed by various visitors to their farmhouse that they even drank whisky out of the teapot.

However, one day a great evangelist came to Jabez and in the midst of revivalist fervour many people were greatly affected by the Holy Spirit. Among those who confessed the errors of their ways were Wally and Llinos, and at the end of the service they went to the front of the chapel with tears running down their faces. Speaking to the packed congregation, with his arms lifted towards Heaven, Wally declared:

"Friends, today my life has been changed. Praise be the Lord! Yes indeed. Wicked ways is a thing of the past. This day, through his infinite grace, He have converted me, He have converted my wife, and He have converted the teapot."

Preaching in Camrose

The minister of a Camrose chapel had been there so long that no one could remember anybody else. In all the years of his ministry he had never allowed anybody else to occupy his pulpit, and he had never missed a Sunday through illness.

On one occasion a young student home from theological college called at the manse and asked the minister if he might be allowed to give the sermon on the following Sunday. "We are told by our Principal", he explained, "that we need practical experience to see how well we are suited to the ministry."

"My dear young man," said the minister, placing a hand on his shoulder, "if I let you preach on Sunday morning and you give a better sermon than me, my congregation would never again be satisfied with my preaching; and if you're not a better preacher than me, you're not worth listening to."

Uncommonly Good Potatoes

It was the month of August, and in spite of the beautiful weather the minister of Tabernacle Chapel had a troubled look on his face as he prepared to launch into his Sunday morning sermon. He gave out his text and then said "Friends, I have found it difficult to expand this text today, as the commentators do not agree with me." Somehow these words lodged in the brain of Freddie Thomas as he sat in the back row, unable to concentrate on the dense exposition that followed.

Next day the minister was in his study in the manse when Freddie knocked at the door. The reverend gentleman was surprised to see that he had with him a large sack of potatoes. "Good gracious, Freddie," he exclaimed, "Is this for me?" "Indeed it is," said Freddie. "I couldn't get it out of me mind what tha' said yesterday about them common taters not agreein' with thee. So I thought to meself, my taters are uncommon good this year. Then I thought I'd better bring thee a bagful so as to set thee to rights again."

A Sacrifice for the Lord

In the 1930s many small country chapels in Pembrokeshire had no ministers of their own, and would have to depend upon lay preachers to conduct many of their Sunday services. Preachers were normally booked for the day, and they would be expected, in return for their travel expenses, to conduct three services, the first at 11 am, the second at 2.30 pm and the third at 6 pm. In between, they would be offered lunch and their afternoon tea, and members of the congregation would pride themselves on their generous hospitality.

Once upon a time a young lay preacher was booked to provide the services at Hill Mountain Chapel near Neyland. Mr and Mrs Rees offered to look after him for the day, and since he had not been to the chapel before they were keen to make a good impression. Mrs Rees missed the morning service because she was cooking a large and delicious lunch of roast beef, Yorkshire pudding and four veg, followed by rice pudding, and then cherry cake and coffee. The young preacher was probably nervous about the afternoon service, and after picking at his food for a while he left most of it on his plate. He saw the disappointment on the faces of his hosts, but offered the excuse that he never could eat before he preached, because it hindered his oratory.

Later on Mr Rees accompanied the preacher to chapel while his wife stayed at home to clear the table and do the washing up. After the service the young man remained at the chapel gate chatting to members of the congregation while Mr Rees returned home to put the kettle on for afternoon tea. Seeing that he was alone, Mrs Rees could not contain her curiosity about the service and the sermon. "Well, William, how did he preach?" she asked.

"Huh!" replied her husband. "'A might as well 'ave ate!"

Enlightenment is at Hand

The little Methodist Chapel at Portfield Gate had to depend for many of its Sunday services upon the goodwill and commitment of various lay preachers. One day the appointed lay preacher fell ill, and so the service had to be taken at very short notice by one of the chapel stewards. All went well with the hymns and prayers, but then came the time for the sermon. Old Billy Evans stood up in the pulpit, shaking with nerves.

"Friends," he said. "This is all a bit new to me, never havin' done no sermonizin' afore. But I'll have a l' bash at it with the help o' the Good Lord. There's many great mysteries for this world that you an' me knows nothin' about. But the Lord knows everythin'! So he is goin' to help me this mornin' - I feels it in me bones - to unscrew the unscrewtable."

Billy and the Kittens

Billy Sharp lived in Portfield, at the top end of Haverfordwest. His prize Persian cat had two kittens, which he wanted to sell. He couldn't find a buyer, but then somebody told him that the minister's cat had been run over, and that he might be looking for a new one. Billy didn't know which minister to approach, so he did the rounds of the clergymen in town. First he went to Father Maguire, and urged him to buy while the price was right, winding up his sales pitch with an assurance that both kittens were good Roman Catholics. The priest was unimpressed, as indeed was every other minister visited over the next few days, even though each in turn was assured that the kittens were good Baptists, Congregationalists, Anglicans or whatever.

At last Billy knocked on the door of the Methodist manse, and when confronted by the minister gave his usual sales pitch, assuring him that the kittens were good Methodists. "Aha, Billy," said the minister. "You're an old rascal. I happen to know Father Maguire very well, and he told me that when you called on him a few days ago you assured him that they were good Roman Catholics."

"That's very true, reverend" replied Billy, with a sudden flash of inspiration. "But that was before their eyes were opened." The minister bought the kittens.

Encouraging the Flock

Once upon a time a new Circuit minister arrived at the little Methodist Chapel at Portfield Gate to officiate at his first service there. All went well until the collection. An old sidesman passed around the offertory plate while the harmonium wheezed out its usual tune, but then the minister was scandalized to see the old fellow quietly taking out a three-penny bit from the plate before handing it over to be blessed. As soon as the service was finished he called the steward to one side and told him, with some emotion, that his little lapse had been observed.

"Oh, don't tha worry about that, reverend," came the reply. "I've been leadin' off with that old three-penny bit of mine these past fifteen years. The little flock just needs a bit of encouragement like, and if the Lord was worried He'd have surely let me know afore now!"

Ministerial Status in Harfat

Three small boys from Honey Harfat were earnestly discussing the abilities of their respective fathers. One of them, who was the son of a "Western Telegraph" journalist, said: "My dad came home the other evening, wrote an article in three hours after supper, and got paid five pounds for it."

The second boy, who was the son of a local photographer, said: "My dad spent a couple of hours taking pictures of an old lady the other day, and got paid ten pounds for it."

The third boy, who was the son of the minister of Wesley Chapel, was at first non-plussed. But then he had a heavenly inspiration. "The other day there was a big do going on in the chapel," he said. "My dad got up in the pulpit and talked for twenty minutes, and afterwards it took twelve men to carry all the money up to him."

Evangelism at Work

Colin Clip-clip was a barber from Neyland who became greatly affected by a religious revival in the town. He was converted from his wicked ways, and with great zeal and joy he determined to do all he could to bring others to the happy condition in which he now found himself. On enquiring of the evangelist how he might best spread the gospel, he was told that all he needed to do to bring others closer to God was to have a few quiet words with all those who came into his barber's shop.

The following morning the first person to come into the shop was Buffy Jenkins, a large and grizzled individual who played prop forward in the town rugby team. "Shave please, Colin," he said as he settled himself into the chair. Colin got him all lathered up, picked up his razor and was about to start the shaving job when he suddenly remembered that he was supposed to do a bit of quiet evangelizing on his customers. Holding the cut-throat razor a few inches in front of Buffy's nose, he asked in sepulchral tones: "Tell me sir, are you prepared to pass through the Gates of Eternity and to meet your maker?"

Like a rocket Buffy shot from the barber's chair, flung the door open and fled down the street, leaving Colin to wonder why the Lord's message had not been better received.

A Peaceful End

Rev Thomas was spending the afternoon at a house in Manorbier, where he had been preaching in the morning service. After tea he was sitting in the lounge with his hosts when their two children came rushing in. "Mum! Dad!" cried young Davy, carrying a large rat in his arms. "Don't be afraid - he's dead. We found him in the corner of the old barn, and beat him with the shovel and bashed him with a piece of wood and chucked a brick at him. Then we stuck the garden fork through him..."

Suddenly the children noticed the gentleman with the dog-collar, and the little girl, with all the skills of the diplomat, added in a grave voice: "And then the Good Lord took him unto Himself."

An Old Friend of the Family

Once upon a time the Pope came to visit Cardiff, and Alderman Albert Evans, the Chairman of Preseli Pembrokeshire District Council, was invited to meet him. Albert was getting on a bit, and he was not renowned for his tact, so before he travelled up to Cardiff to meet the Holy Father, Dicky Howells the PR man took him to one side for a briefing. "Mind now," said Dicky, "you must always remember to address him correctly, and mind you don't put your foot in it." "Don't you worry," replied Albert, "I have met a Pope once before, when I was a kid. I knows the form all right."

So when he was introduced to His Holiness, Albert shook his outstretched hand and said "Pleased to meet you, sir. I had the pleasure of knowing your holy father, the late Pope. And I hope the wife is keepin' well."

Chapter Six

WORKERS AND BOSSES

Cooling Off

Ezekiel Evans was a hard-working employee of Haverfordwest Town Council, and once upon a time he was employed with the rest of his gang to dig a big trench down High Street to take a new water main. Shortly before noon one day the big boss from the council offices came buy, and noticed that Ezekiel was lying on his back in the sun smoking a cigarette, with his redundant shovel stuck into a pile of earth.

"Evans!" shouted the boss. "What do you mean, lying on your back at this time of day when you should be hard at work? That shovel is meant to be used!"

"Sorry sir," replied Ezekiel. "But I've already shifted three tons this mornin' since I started work, an' me shovel was gettin' so hot it was startin' to melt in me hands. I had to give it a rest so as to cool it off."

Qualified for the Job

In the good old days when Pembrokeshire County Council ran the schools of the county, the Chairman of the Education Committee was one Cllr Emlyn Jones. He was so illiterate that he couldn't read even the clearest handwriting. At one committee meeting a new clerk came in and delivered a letter relating to an important agenda item, and he noticed that, after opening it, Cllr Jones was holding it upside down and scanning it intently. "Excuse me, Alderman Jones," said the clerk meekly, "but if I may say so you are holding the letter the wrong way up." This caused great embarrassment among the committee members, but the Chairman was equal to the occasion.
"Now look ye here, young man," he said haughtily, "do ye think I could have got up to this here elevated position as Chairman of the Educatin' Committee if I couldn't read a letter upside down, or come to that, with any side up whatsoever?"

Come Back Tomorrow

Ronnie Reynish from Dale was looking for a job when they were building the council houses in Marloes. The foreman was a local man, and after an exhaustive interview he concluded by saying:

"Well now Ronnie, I can't start thee today, but if tha comes back tomorrow I might be able to give thee a job. The position is a bit confusin' on account of the labour situation. You see, we has too many on the books, except that we are a bit understaffed indeed. For example, I has a fella here today who hasn't turned up. So I'll tell thee what. If a doesn't come tomorrow, I'll send'n home and tha canst have his job."

A Job for Life

Jabez James worked in the coal-yard near the Old Bridge in Haverfordwest. He was not the fastest of workers, and one day the boss came up to him and told him that he would have to dispense with his services.

"Indeed that is a very great disappointment to me, boss," said Jabez. "With my great knowledge of the business I had it in me mind that this was a nice little job for life."

"Don't be ridiculous!" shouted the boss. "You know next to nothing about the business, and quite frankly I will be better off without you."

"Suit yerself, boss," said Jabez, calm as you like. "But I knows enough to be a very handy chap for Rees Brothers Coal Merchants up in Portfield. For example, I knows perfectly well after all the learnin' I've done that down here by the Old Bridge seventeen hundredweight makes a ton, and that a hundredweight of water weighs as much as a hundredweight of coal." Jabez kept his job.

Emergency Measures

Once upon a time there was a terrible fire at the Texaco Refinery not far from Pembroke. The company's own fire fighters were at full stretch, and the County Fire Brigade had all available fire-fighting teams at the scene of the fire. The inferno was out of control, and a call went out for all other fire-fighting equipment in West Wales to rush to the scene. Harry Herbert from Neyland, who had bought a second-hand fire engine a few years earlier, heard of the SOS and decided that there might be an opportunity to earn a few quid. So he threw an assortment of fire-fighting odds and ends into his vehicle, gathered up a few friends, and rushed off over the Cleddau Bridge.

Much to the amazement of the assembled fire-fighters, Harry's fire-engine came roaring down the refinery road, screeched round the corner and headed straight for the fiery inferno without stopping for instructions. With mounting horror the professional firemen watched from a safe distance as the vehicle went straight into the middle of the fire at fifty mph. Five or six figures leapt out, wrapped handkerchiefs around their faces, and started beating out the flames with their jackets and with old hessian potato sacks. They worked like men possessed, with Harry rushing about like a demon and throwing buckets of water in all directions.

Then, suddenly and miraculously, the flames died down and the fire went out. A great cheer went up from the assembled firemen and refinery workers, and Harry and his mates were given a hero's reception as they staggered, singed and smoke-covered, up towards the refinery office. Then, after a moving speech, the refinery manager wrote out a cheque for £50,000 and presented it to Harry as a gesture of appreciation from the company.

Later on, after receiving medical treatment, a good meal and new clothes all round, Harry and his friends were given a lift home in a company car. On the way, Harry turned to his mates and whispered: "Hells bells, boys, that was a bit too close for comfort. We **must** get them bloody brakes fixed!"

A Hard Night

Cuthbert lived on the council estate in Marloes, and he worked on a local farm as a cow-hand. One day he turned up for work looking terrible, and during the milking the farmer noticed that he was more asleep than awake. "You are looking pretty rough today, Cuthbert," said the farmer. "What's the matter?"

"I've had a terrible time," replied Cuthbert. "Up half the night, I was."

"What was the trouble?"

"It was that wretched cat," said Cuthbert. "I was sittin' up in the kitchen till three o'clock, waitin' for her to come in so that I could put her out for the night."

How to be Upwardly Mobile

Mr Sidney Bowler had a big grocery shop in High Street in Haverfordwest. It was a busy and successful business, having grown from very modest beginnings. According to legend, when the business was very young the staff consisted of Mr Bowler himself and a fourteen-year-old lad who did the deliveries.

One day the lad came to Mr Bowler and said "Sir, I feels ashamed goin' to all your customers lookin' so tatty. Me trousers is full of holes, and there's hardly nothin' left of me shoes. Me poor ol' Mam an' Dad haven't got a penny to spare, so what am I to do?"

Mr Bowler was greatly moved by this plea from the heart, and so he gave the boy a guinea from his modest savings, telling him to go out and get some new clothes and shoes.

Next day the boy was absent from work, but in the evening Mr Bowler met his mother on the street and enquired whether he was unwell. "No no, Mr Bowler," she replied. "A's very well thank you. Indeed, thanks to you a was lookin' so smart this mornin' that I thought I'd better send'n round town to see if a could get himself a better job."

The New Boss

Thomas, Jones, Williams & Co was an old-established building firm in Pembroke Dock which fell upon hard times. It was taken over by a rival firm called Evans, Davies, Hughes & Co. Mr Meredith Evans was the brash and energetic boss of the newly combined company, and he determined that he would knock the work-force of TJW into shape so that they could make a proper contribution to the profits of the new organization. One day he made an unannounced visit to a building site in the dockyard town where the TJW workers were completing a housing contract. He found a number of things which he didn't approve of, and decided that decisive action was needed. So he summoned the foreman and said to him "Jim, there are a number of things here that have to be put right. There are too many bricks lying about, the timber needs to be covered over, and the concrete mixer is in a terrible state. And by the way, I have just caught a fellow hanging about by the shed, smoking during working hours. I sacked him on the spot, told the girl in the office to give him a week's wages and saw him off the site.".

"Very good, Mr Evans, sir," said the foreman with a grin. "I knows all about it, for I seen the man leavin' a few minutes past. That was Tommy James from Pennar, who just called in on the off-chance to see if I could give 'n a job."

Small Incident on the Haven Road

Once upon a time, not very long ago, an elderly spinster lived in a tidy bungalow on the Haven Road in Haverfordwest. She was a faithful member of Bethesda Chapel, and led a sheltered, comfortable and God-fearing life. One day two GPO workmen had occasion to repair a fault on a telephone pole outside her home. Bill was up the pole mending the wires, and Tommy was on the ground below, sorting out the tools for the job. Suddenly the elderly spinster was shocked to hear a string of expletives, some of which she had never heard before and others were distinctly blasphemous. She remonstrated with the men and later wrote a letter of complaint to the local GPO manager.

The manager called the culprits into his office and asked for their version of events. "Well, sir," said Tommy, "It were like this. Me an' Bill was on the job, fixin' the line. A was up the pole an' I was down below findin' them wire cutters from the bag. Then Billy let some hot lead drip on me head and dropped his heavy hammer on me foot. So I said to 'n as tidy as you like: Now then, you really must be more careful, William."

The Workmen of Trecwn

Many of the operations undertaken at the Royal Naval Armaments Depot at Trecwn were shrouded in secrecy, and there was some doubt locally about the size of the work-force. One of the standard replies to the question "How many men work at Trecwn?" was "On a good day, about half of them."

Rumour has it that a cameraman from the Royal Navy once visited the depot with a new-fangled movie camera. He was shooting some location film from a lane along the Trecwn valley, and happened to meet an old farmer. Keen to show himself as friendly to the natives, the cameraman said: "Good afternoon, sir. I have just been taking some moving pictures of life in the armaments depot with this special camera."

"Well well, there's nice," said the old farmer. "And did you catch any of the men moving?"

"Oh, indeed I did," came the reply.

The farmer shook his head reflectively. "Science is a wonderful thing," he said slowly, and went on his way.

The Art of Energy Conservation

A farm labourer from Wiston was seeking work at the Portfield hiring fair. He got into conversation with a Rudbaxton farmer, and assured him that never, in any circumstances, did he get tired.

"Aha!" said the farmer. "There are not many of your kind about. You are just the sort of man I want. You have got yourself a job."

A couple of days later, whilst riding along a leafy lane on his land, the farmer came across the new farmhand, who was supposed to be hedge-trimming. The boss was surprised to see him flat out on his back in the shade of a great oak tree, dozing contentedly as the air was filled with bird-song.

"What's this?" cried the farmer. "I thought you said you never got tired?"

"Well now," replied the labourer, rubbing his eyes. "No more I don't. But I pretty soon would, master, if I didn't have a bit of a rest now and again."

It Runs in the Family

Bert worked in a district council depot in Neyland. He was a good worker, but the depot manager noticed that he was regularly late for work on Thursday mornings. He called Bert into his office for a good ticking-off, and having done that he asked him why it was that he could never get up in time for work on Thursday mornings.

"Funny you should mention it, boss," said Bert. "I was just discussin' this very thing with me mates a couple of days ago. You see, I goes out for to play darts, quite regular like, on Wednesday evenin's in the 'Rose and Crown'. After the game me and the lads has a few pints and then we goes home. But the funny thing is, boss, that I always sleeps very slowly on Wednesday nights. I do believe it runs in the family.

Shareholder's Privilege

Two small boys were walking across Salutation Square in Haverfordwest. Ivor was ten years old and Charlie was eight. "Hey," said Ivor. "I've got a farthin'. Have you got a farthin', Charlie?" "I got one too", said Charlie.

"Then why don't we got to Mr Morse Tobacconist an' get a ha'penny-worth o' Woodbines?" Charlie agreed with this fine scheme, and by pooling their resources the boys bought half of a Woodbine cigarette. Ivor lit up the evil weed and puffed away happily for a while as the two boys walked up the High Street. Eventually Charlie got frustrated.

"Now then, Ivor," he said. "Isn't it about time I had a smoke too?"

"Shut up", said Ivor. "I'm the chairman of this company, and you are only a shareholder. I'll smoke the fag, an' you can spit."

Chapter Seven

UPSTAIRS, DOWNSTAIRS

A Job for the Young Master

The Squire of Sealyham Mansion had a teenage son, who was known around the estate to be extremely lazy. However, the squire was apparently unaware of his son's exceptional capacity for inactivity, and thought him to be a hard worker and a worthy heir to the family fortune. He was keen for the lad to learn as much as possible about the working and management of the estate, and arranged for him to be taken under the wing of various members of the staff for a few weeks at a time. He worked in the secretary's office, the farm and the kitchen, and the time came for a spell under the head gardener. Old Joseph was not amused, having heard of the problems which his colleagues had had with the young master. "Look after him well," said the squire, "and teach him all you know". "What I knows took me sixty years to learn," grumbled Joseph, "so a won't get far in a couple o' weeks. But don't tha worry, squire, I'll learn the lad somethin' that'll come in nice 'n handy for the future."

A week later the squire was doing his rounds of the estate when he met Joseph in the garden. "And how's the lad getting on?" he asked. "Top class, squire," replied the old man. "The young master's a bit slow, but there's one job a's wonderful at. If tha goes down to the croquet lawn just now tha'll see'n hard at work, roundin' up the snails."

The Art of Diplomacy

Squire Owen of Maesgwynne had been abroad for six months, visiting the museums of the capital cities of Europe. When he returned he was met at Clynderwen railway station by Tom Jenkins, an old family servant. After settling

himself in the carriage for the last leg of the journey home through the leafy lanes of the estate, the squire said "Well, Tom how are things at Maesgwynne?"

"Not too bad, master, but I has to tell thee that there is an uncommon lot of rabbits on the estate this year." "That's most unfortunate. And why should that be, Tom?"

"They do say, master, that it is on account of the fact that the old dog has died."

"Is poor Felix dead?" asked the squire. "Dear me, that is a pity. How did he die?"

"Very bad business it was, Sir. It must have been the roof of the burnin' barn that fell on him."

"Good gracious! Has the barn burned down? How on earth did that happen?"

"We ain't too sure of that, Sir. But they do say that it must have been a spark from the burnin' of the great house that set if off."

"Merciful heavens! You don't mean to say that the house was on fire too?"

"Burnt to the ground it was. But don't get upset, master; it was only just a little fire at first."

"How terrible, Tom! And how did it happen?"

"They do say that it was nothing serious, exceptin' that the old lady, your mother - God rest her soul in Heaven - must have dropped a lighted candle somewhere in the parlour."

Neither Forward nor Backward

On one of her visits to Pembrokeshire Lady Hamilton was accompanied by Lord Nelson and his personal servant Davy Jones. Davy was a Pembrokeshire man who knew all Nelson's secrets but who was a model of discretion. Davy went to great pains to unload the great lady's personal luggage from the coach and to carry it to her room. She observed his attentiveness and felt inclined to reward him in some way.

"Now then, my friend," she said, "what will you have to drink?"

"Why, please, me Lady, I do declare I'm not thirsty."

"But," said her ladyship, "Nelson's man must drink with me, so what will you take, a dram, a glass of grog, a glass of punch?"

"Well indeed," replied Davy, "as I'm to drink with yer ladyship's honour, it wouldn't be good manners to be forward, an' it'd be even worse manners to be backward, so I'll take the dram now, and will be drinkin' the glass of grog while yer ladyship is mixin' the tumbler of punch for me."

Finding a Gardener

The master of a big house near Hayscastle found himself a charming young wife. The new mistress had much to learn about the running of the household, but she recognized her own inexperience and was keen to take the advice of others.

One of her tasks was to find a new gardener to look after the grounds, and she advertised the post in the "West Wales Guardian". There were two applicants for the job, and by coincidence they both turned up for interview at the same time.

The young mistress talked to Harry first, but he was a shy fellow who did not make a good impression. Then she talked to Jenkin, who was a confident and fluent talker. The mistress was about to offer the job to Jenkin when she spied the old housekeeper in the porch behind the men. She was gesturing frantically towards Harry, making it perfectly clear as to her preference. The mistress decided to take the old lady's advice, and gave the job to Harry. Afterwards she asked the housekeeper why she seemed so certain in her mind that the one applicant was so much better than the other.

"Well, ma'am," she replied. "I has learnt meself over the years that when lookin' for a gardener you looks at his corduroys. Harry has his patches on the knees, which is where you likes to see 'em. But as for that Jenkin - he has his patches on his bum!"

The New Maid

Mrs Edwards from the big house in Llawhaden had got a new maid. The girl was somewhat slow on the uptake, and her work was distinctly slovenly. Having warned her many times about jobs undone or poorly done, Mrs Edwards said she would give her one last chance to show that she was worthy of her post.

Next morning Annie was cleaning the parlour, having already dealt with the dining-room to her satisfaction. Mrs Edwards made a quick check and shouted: "Annie! Just come into the dining-room for a moment. I want to show you something." Annie obediently hurried in from the parlour.

"Now look at this," continued the lady of the house angrily. "Just watch me. When I move my finger like this I can write my name in the dust on the dining table. So what do you have to say about that?"

"There's wonderful, Madam," replied Annie with an appreciative smile. "It jest goes to show what a bit o' schoolin' can do for you."

Getting Started in Business

Arthur Reynolds was starting a new shop in Narberth, and was in the process of laying in new stock. One day he had to go into Haverfordwest for some shop fittings, and left Maria in charge. She was new to the job, so he explained to her that she must be very civil to various gentlemen who might call, since they were the representatives of the companies with whom he would be doing much important business. Off he went, and when he returned late in the afternoon he asked Maria how she had got on.

"Oh very well, Mr Reynolds," she replied. "Nine or ten very smart gentlemen called when you were out. But it was a funny thing. Every one of them said "Would you like to take my card?" I knew very well that you have got plenty of cards of your own, just new from the printers, so I told them no thank you very much. Some of them got quite upset, but one can understand it I suppose, since it must be very irritating to come all this way from London only to find that you have got your cards already from the Guardian office."

Good Breeding in Tenby

For over one hundred and fifty years the restaurants of Tenby have been renowned for the quality of their service. In some of the old-established hotels the waiters have learned over the years to accept the dictum that the customer is always right, and thus deserves to be treated with dignity. One day a resident of the "Royal Gatehouse" hotel came down to breakfast, and the following conversation occurred.

"Good morning, Sir! God morning, madam! I trust that you both slept well, and that you are full of the joys of life this beautiful morning?"

"Two orange juice, not too strong, each with one lump of ice and diluted with 25 per cent aerated mineral water."

"Certainly, sir."

"Two bowls of Kelloggs cornflakes with chilled semi-skimmed milk, each sprinkled with two teaspoons of demerara sugar."

"Of course, Sir."

"Two eggs poached medium soft, on wholemeal bread sliced not too thick and toasted not too hard, buttered with soya margarine. Two cups of coffee medium roasted, no sugar, not too much cream."
"
Yes indeed, sir. And would sir like to specify any particular design on the crockery?"

A Quick Walk Home

In the latter years of the Nineteenth Century sedan chairs were still widely used in Haverfordwest. Many members of the Pembrokeshire gentry kept town houses in the county town, and during the social season the place was alive with gossip, parties, meetings and sporting events. The sedan chairs were used for transporting the ladies and gentlemen back and forth between their houses and the inns and meeting rooms, and the carriers belonged to a hardy breed toughened by years of climbing the steep streets with heavy loads.

During Hunt Week the town was particularly busy, and the highlight of the social calendar was the Hunt Ball held in the Assembly Rooms. The rooms were ablaze with coloured lights and sparkling with the beautiful dresses worn by the ladies of the county's social elite. The gaiety of the proceedings was often enhanced by the presence of officers in uniform. The carriages were rolling all night, and the sedan chairs did a roaring trade. Tom Morse and his brother Charlie, Georgy Summers, Georgy Edwards, Jimmy Harries, and George and Johnny Dainty were on the trot half the night.

On one famous occasion, having safely delivered all their clients to the Hunt Ball, the carriers passed their time pleasantly doing the rounds of the Three Tuns, the Black Bear and the Bells. In fact, they swore that they were enjoying themselves no less merrily than their aristocratic patrons in the Ball nearby. When the time came to collect their patrons and deliver them home, Tom and Charlie Morse had had a few too many, and it transpired that their first customer was a large lady, elegantly attired in an elaborate sequinned dress. They fitted her into their sedan chair with some difficulty, and off they went, puffing and panting their erratic way up High Street. Half way up the street, the floor fell out of the sedan chair and the occupant uttered a piercing scream. Tom and Charlie pressed on regardless, with the large lady inside the sedan chair forced to walk along in step with her bearers. No matter how much she screamed and shouted, she could not get them to stop. At last they reached the front door of her town house, and the lady stepped out of the chair, dishevelled and exhausted.

"You wretched fellows!" she shouted. "I have had to walk all the way home inside that contraption of yours! Didn't you hear me screaming and shouting?"

"Dear me, madam," replied Charlie. "I thought the chair got a bit lighter half-way up the street, but I thought it were on account of me and Tom gettin' our second wind. An' if tha said somethin' to us, madam, I do declare we heard not a thing, on account of the wind blowin' in the wrong direction."

Too Late by Far

Mrs Williams, the doctor's wife, had an attractive young maid called Mari. One day she called Mari into the parlour and said to her "Mari, I saw the milkman kiss you this morning on the front door-step. In future I will take the milk in myself."

"It wouldn't do you no good, madam," replied Mari. "The milkman have promised never to kiss anybody but me."

No Place for Ernie

Life was hard in Pembrokeshire during the dark days of the Second World War. One day two elderly gentlemen named Ernie and Ted were walking across Guildhall Square in Tenby when they saw a sign which read "Economical

Cooking - Demonstration in Progress". They decided to pop in to see what they could learn. They watched fascinated as the lady demonstrator showed how to cook eggless puddings and butter-less cakes. And then she said: "I will now tell you how a splendid soup can be made for next to nothing. First of all, take the bones left over from the Sunday joint...."

"Come on, Ted," said Ernie suddenly, "this ain't no place for us." And with that he dragged his friend from the hall.

Outside Ted said: "What's the matter, Ernie? Don't you like soup?"

"Oh aye," replied Ernie. "I likes soup well enough. But how many bones do she think there is in half a slice o' blood puddin?"

Polite to the Last

Miss Smith was an old widowed lady who moved to Tenby between the Wars for the sake of her health. She had a young maid named Jenny who lived in and looked after her in her ailing years. One cold winter Miss Smith fell ill with the pneumonia, and her condition caused the doctor some concern. She began to recover, but in view of her age the doctor was keen to keep a check on her progress.

"Now then, young lady," he said one day to Jenny, "I want you to call over and see me every morning to let me know about Miss Smith's condition. I think she's getting better, but I need to know how she slept, what her appetite is like, and so forth."

For several days the maid called on the doctor, gave Miss Smith's compliments, and reported on her condition. The doctor felt that the old lady's recovery was well on the way, but then Jenny called in on her regular visit to the surgery and said:

"Good morning, sir. Miss Smith sends her compliments, and she died last night at eight o'clock."

Easing in Gently

Mrs Edwardes of Sealyham Mansion had employed a new maid, and she was giving her a training session as to her duties. After running over all manner of things with the girl, she concluded: "And finally, Hannah, we have breakfast at eight o'clock sharp."

"Very well, Ma'am," replied Hannah. " After all these hundreds of jobs to do I shall probably be sleepin' very sound. If I ain't down by eight just you carry on without me. I'll have mine when I wakes up."

An Educated Man

Mr Allen-Moorhouse from the big house in Angle was looking for a new man to help out on the estate. So he went along to the village and met a peasant on the main street. "I say, my good man," said the lord of the manor, "I am looking for a man to help out on the estate, three days a week. Might you be interested in the position I'm offering?"

"Well sir, that depends, like," replied George. "I has a lot of commitments, what with a wife an' five youngsters to feed."

"Don't think too long," said the gentleman, "or I shall look elsewhere."

"Consider me available for interview, sir. I am a educated fellow, an' honest as they comes, an' no responsibility is too great for me to carry on me broad shoulders. An' I am a hell of a worker, once I gives me commitment."

"Very well," said Mr Allen-Moorhouse. "I am in a hurry, so let's have a little interview here and now. Let's just see what your general knowledge is like. Now then, how many days are there in a year?"

"Seven, sir," replied George.

"Seven? But everybody should know that there are 365 days in a year."

"Ah yes, sir, but that would be cheatin'. The days in the year is Sunday, Monday, Tuesday, Wednesday, Thursday, Friday and Saturday. Bein' a honest man, I considers it to be most irregular to count these days more than the once."

Chapter Eight

THE JOYS OF MARRIAGE

Posh Wedding in Goodwick

Not long ago there were two Pembrokeshire ladies named Mrs Davies and Mrs Jones. They who lived in the same street, just a few doors apart, in the north Pembrokeshire village of Goodwick. One of them had a most attractive daughter called Mair. She was very eligible, and only nineteen years old.

One day Mrs Jones and Mrs Davies met down at the post office, where they were picking up their Social Security money. "Good morning Mrs Jones bach," said Mrs Davies. "How are you then?"

"Very well indeed, thank you, bach," said Mrs Jones. "And have you heard our news?"

"Oh, what's that?" asked Mrs Davies, all interest.

"Our Mair is getting married."

"Oooh, there's nice," said Mrs Davies. "And when is the baby due?"

"Don't be disgusting," replied Mrs Jones, looking down her nose. "Babies has got nothing to do with it."

Mrs Davies looked suitably impressed. "Ooooh, there's posh," she said.

Ingenuity in Letterston

Penry Morris was a short man, five foot nothing in his bare feet, and known universally as Morris Minor in his home village of Letterston. His friends and neighbours were amazed one day when he announced his engagement to a very large Australian lady named Marlene, who stood six foot two in her nylons. There was great speculation as to his sexual prospects, and everybody predicted disaster. However, the wedding came and went, and as the months went by everybody noticed that Penry was thriving, and so was his gorgeous wife.

The gossip in "The Harp" turned to sexual techniques, and Davy and Llew decided to investigate. One evening, when Penry and Marlene were throwing a party in their house, the lads found some pretext to creep upstairs and investigate the bedroom. They searched high and low, but all they could find was a large galvanized bucket standing in the corner. Next time they met Penry in the pub they came clean about their nefarious mission. "Very sorry to disturb your matrimonial bliss, Penry bach," said Llew, "but me and the lads are very keen to know the secret of your happy married life. Damn and blast -- all we could find in your bedroom was a bucket in the corner."

"Well boys, " replied Penry with a gleam in his eye, "I'll tell you a little secret about that bucket. Got it in the Clynderwen Farmers' sex shop in Croesgoch, I did. When Marlene is in the mood, I puts it over her head and swings from the handle."

Relative Values

Idris was coming up to his twenty-fifth birthday, and thought it was probably time he got married and settled down. There were many beautiful girls in Clynderwen, but he was madly in love with the fair Mari, who lived next door. So he went to his father and informed him that he wanted to marry Mari. "Very sorry, son," said his father, "but that's impossible. You see, Mari is actually your sister."

Dismayed at this revelation, Idris fell in love with Morfydd instead; and a few weeks later reported to his father the fact that he had set his heart on marrying her. "You mean Morfydd who works in the Farmers Co-op?" said the old man. "Oh dear. Afraid not, boyo, for she is your sister as well."

Undeterred, Idris set off on another trail and fell in love with Blodwen from down by the railway. He went to his father again to seek his blessing on a marriage -- with exactly the same result as before. Now poor Idris really was distraught, and moped about the house for several days. At last his mother said to him: "What's wrong, son? It wouldn't be girl trouble by any chance, would it?" "Afraid so, Mam," replied Idris. "Every time I go to Dad and tell him I want to marry somebody in the village he tells me its impossible. It looks to me as if they are all sisters of mine."

"Don't you worry about that, Idris bach," came the reply. "That silly old fool who thinks he's your Dad is no relation of yours anyway."

The Dreadful Secret

Glyn and Catrin both lived in Puncheston, and everybody in the village was delighted when they announced their engagement to be married. On the day before the wedding Catrin said to Glyn: "Cariad, before we get married there is something dreadful about my past life that I must tell you." "No, no," replied Glyn. "I love you the way you are, and I don't want to know anything about your past. If you must, tell me after we are married."

After the wedding, when the happy couple were on their way to Wolfscastle for their honeymoon, Catrin tried to raise the matter of her dreadful secret again. "I won't hear of it," said Glyn. "But if you insist you can tell me when we are in bed together; that'll be soon enough."

So that night as they got into bed together Catrin finally revealed her secret. "I have to tell you, Glyn bach," she said, "that I am still a virgin." Glyn was flabbergasted. He let out a mighty yell, leaped out of bed, put all his clothes back on and said: "This is terrible! I have to go back and talk to mother about this!" And with that he rushed out of the hotel, leaving poor Catrin weeping in the bridal bed.

When he got home his mother exclaimed: "Good God, Glyn! What are you doing here? I thought you was on your honeymoon?"

"So I was, Mam. But things will never work out. I have had to leave Catrin, for it seems she is a virgin."

"Well I never!" said his Mam. "Who would have thought it! What a disgrace on the family. But you did quite right, bach. If that there Catrin Evans is not good enough for the rest of the village she's not good enough for you."

Making an Effort

Billy John from Llangwm was a splendid fellow and a new member of the local rugby team, back in the days when they used to win matches. He had been courting Kathy from Hook for several years, and at last he plucked up the courage to ask her to marry him. "Most kind of you to ask," said Kathy, "and I am inclined to say yes. But to be honest with you, Billy, I have a bit of a problem with you. Since you took up playin' rugby, your bodily odours on a Saturday night are very nasty indeed. So I'll say yes, but only on condition that you starts to smell a bit fresher. I wants you to promise that every day from now on you'll have a nice bath and put on plenty of deodorant and toilet water." Billy promised faithfully that he would do anything for his beloved, and as he took his leave he promised that when next they met, on Saturday night, be would be smelling fresh as a dew-covered daisy.

When Saturday night came the couple met as usual outside the Hook post office, and Kathy was amazed to see that Billy's head was covered with bandages. "Oh Billy," she exclaimed. "What on earth have you done? Did some horrible rugby player from Neyland jump on your head in the match?"

"Nothin' so simple," replied Billy. "After the match I went home, had me supper, and had a nice bath. Then I put on the deodorant like you said. But then when I was splashin' on the toilet water the toilet seat fell on me head."

Loving Advice

During the Second World War a terrible air raid was taking place in Pembroke Dock. A husband and wife who lived in Church Street thought they had better take evasive action, so they ran down the garden towards their air raid shelter. Just as they reached the entrance the wife stopped in her tracks and said: "Oooh, Willie, I've forgot my false teeth! Hang on a minute while I goes back to the house to fetch them."

"Don't be dull, maid," said Willie as he dragged her into the air raid shelter. "It's bombs them Germans is droppin' on us, not buns."

No Doubt About It

A famous medium was giving a public demonstration of her wonderful talent in the Pater Hall in Pembroke Dock. The hall was packed, and after various impressive contacts with the spirit world she had the audience in the palm of her hand.

Then, after an impressive silence she went into a trance and said in a weird voice: "I feel a presence in our midst! Yes! Yes! I have a message. Let me see....... Now it's clearer. Yes! It is a message for someone in our audience here tonight. There is somebody here who shops at the co-op every Friday. Now I see a car with a dent in the back. And the car will not start. Now there are twenty pairs of unused shoes, and a wardrobe full of beautiful and expensive clothes. Now I hear voices, lots of voices, going on and on........ Now I see a mouse on the kitchen floor, and I hear a scream. Now I see a football match on the television ... and now it's gone. The screen has gone blank. I see a couple in bed, and one of them has a headache. Oh dear, things are fading....."

And then, after a long and agonizing pause, the medium concluded: "The pictures have gone. Is there anybody here who identifies with the things I have seen? For whom is the message from the spirit world intended?"

And with one accord every single man in the audience stood up and shouted; "Yes! Yes! It's my wife!"

Conversation in Llangwm

The following conversation was once heard on the main street in Llangwm, with one old lady talking to her neighbour.

"Hast tha heard the news?"

"No indeed. Tell me what."

"Mary Jones is gettin' married."

"Gettin' married! In a hurry?"

"Aye aye maid. In a great hurry."

"Blessed Lord! I never knew she was large. Who bigged her?"

Modern Marriage

Justin and Claire were a thoroughly trendy young couple who worked in the tax office in Haverfordwest. They had been living together for some months before they got married, but they had a good wedding in the Registry Office followed by a most splendid wedding reception.

Three days after the wedding one of the wedding guests was walking along Bridge Street when he met Justin coming the other way. "Well hello, Justin," he said. "What are you doing in town? I thought you were away on your honeymoon?"

"Of course I am," replied the young bridegroom. "We are having a modern honeymoon. Claire is down in Torquay visiting her old boy-friend James for a week, and when she comes back I'm having a week in Tenerife with Wendy, just to remind me of old times."

How to be a Good Wife

Brynmor lived up in Puncheston, and as a bachelor was inclined to live beyond his means. Then he got married, and he and his new wife were allocated a house on the council estate. Bethan was determined to get the family finances on a firm footing, much to the disgust of Brynmor.

One day about a month after the wedding Brynmor was working out in the back garden when Bethan called out from the kitchen door:

"Bryn bach, come on in for a little break from plantin' the spuds. Your tea's ready - poached eggs on toast, bara brith an' Welsh cakes as usual."

Brynmor dropped his spade in astonishment, for this had not happened before, and ran into the kitchen. "Now then, Bethan bach, you must be kiddin' me," he said.

"No, no, Bryn," replied the good wife. "It ain't you I'm kiddin', it's the neighbours. We has to establish our credentials."

The Minister in Trouble

Betsy Jones was a ferocious and tough lady who lived in the Gwaun Valley with her hen-pecked husband Joseph. The poor man had a hard time of it, and the neighbours wondered how he put up with her tantrums and constant nagging. According to a wicked rumour, which is probably untrue, Betsy stormed one day into the Baptist manse and confronted the minister. "Reverend bach", she shouted, "did you or did you not marry me and that layabout Joseph all them years ago?"

"Of course I did, Betsy," replied the minister. "I remember it well."

"Well then," she screamed, "what are you goin' to do about it? He's escaped!"

Dai's Aeroplane Flight

In the early days of aviation it was something very special to go up in an aeroplane. Dai lived near St David's in the 1920s, and he became friendly with a pilot who had learnt his skills during the Great War. The pilot got himself a new aeroplane and made frequent trips to Dublin, and one day Dai asked him if he and his wife might join him on a flight to Ireland. The pilot thought for a while, and then said "All right, Dai. But you must realise that modern flying is a very complicated business and that the pilot needs total concentration. You are a good friend, but you talk too much. I'll take you and your wife to Dublin on condition that you say not a word to me until we land on the other side." Dai agreed, and on the appointed day off they went, winging their way westwards across St George's Channel. The pilot was in the cockpit, with Dai and his wife behind.

When they landed at Dublin the pilot turned round and asked Dai if he had enjoyed the flight.

"Grand, grand," replied Dai. "I never thought that flying was such fun."

The pilot then congratulated Dai on keeping silent for so long.

"Quite hard it was, man," said Dai, "especially when you looped the loop out over the water, and Mattie fell out o' the machine."

Survival of the Cautious

John Piccadilly had moved away from Pembrokeshire to London as a young man, and now, in his sixties, he came back to Carew to visit his old haunts. He happened to be passing the graveyard, and saw a lady placing some flowers on a grave. In spite of the passing of the years he recognized her at once as an old flame, and struck up a conversation with her. She was pleased to see him, and they reminisced about old times. Then she told him that she was decorating the grave of her late husband George, who had died six months before.

Johnny noticed that there were three other bunches of flowers on the grass at her side, and asked if they were also intended for the graves of relatives. "Yes indeed," she replied. "These are for my other three husbands - Albert, Tom and Henry - all buried here in the graveyard, side by side." Johnny was surprised to say the least, and expressed his sadness at the lady's string of misfortunes.

"Ah," said the lady pensively, surveying the row of graves, "if only you'd had more courage, you might have been among them!"

Small Talk in Pembroke Dock

Daisy and Maisie lived in a tidy terrace not far from the Dockyard in Pembroke Dock. One day they were chatting over the garden wall.

"Did you hear about that Maggie Jenkins?" said Daisy. "In the family way again."

"Yes, I heard," replied Maisie. She told me herself. Talk, talk, talk! I couldn't get a word in sideways, and got quite hoarse listenin' to her."

"They tells me," said Daisy, "that you're workin' day and night since you was up before the magistrate for beatin' up your husband."

"Yes indeed. His honour said if I came before him again he'd fine me a quid."

"Well well. So you're workin' flat out to keep out o' mischief?"

"Don't be daft," said Maisie. "I'm workin' day and night to save up the quid."

Dire Consequences

Willy Whisky was a stonemason who lived up Letterston way. Unfortunately he was in the habit of getting drunk every Saturday night, with consequent misery to his wife Ann Eliza. The local minister had often rebuked him and told him that if he did not mend his ways he would be condemned to a life hereafter of fire and brimstone. It did no good, and at last, in desperation. Ann Eliza went to consult Dr Harries, the magician who lived in Dinas. When she returned she said to Willy "Now then, husband, I been to see the good doctor, and he says to tell you that if ever you come home drunk again, he'll turn you into a rat."

Willy was considerably frightened by this threat, and for a couple of months he managed to keep sober. But then, one Saturday night, he came home rolling drunk and in great distress.

"Ann Eliza, he wailed, falling onto his knees and weeping into her apron, "I'm drunk again, I'm mortal drunk, and I know the good doctor will see me in his magic mirror! He'll turn me into a rat any minute now. When ye sees me gettin' littler and littler, and the hair comin' out all over me, and a tail comin' on to me, for God's sake, Ann Eliza, turn out the cat."

Small Talk in Neyland

Mary Jane and Daisy Bosom met up on the main street in Neyland.

"Good morning, Daisy," said Mary Jane. "How are you today? Lovely wedding it was on Saturday."

"Yes indeed. There's beautiful the bride looked."

"Lovely dress. Nice young man the bridegroom was too. But it was a bad job about his mother."

"Very bad. First time I've ever heard the groom's mother weep louder than the bride's mother. People was most offended."

"Well, what do you expect? They do say she's a Methodist."

A Cure for the Toothache

Jones Casnewydd met his friend Ifans Penrallt in the market square in Fishguard., "Good day to you, Mr Ifans bach!" he said. "And how are you this fine day?"

"Very bad indeed, thank you," replied Mr Ifans. "I am on my way to the dentist, for I'm nearly mad with the toothache."

"Oh, is that all?" said Mr Jones. "Don't you worry, now then. I have a wonderful cure for you, my friend. When I gets the toothache, the first thing I do is to knock off work and buy a bottle of whisky and a lemon. Then I goes home and says to my wife "Blodwen, cariad, put the kettle on." When the kettle is boiled she makes me a couple of mugs of punch; then I gets in the big armchair in front of the fire and puts my wife on my knee. Then I rests my jaw where the toothache is against her breast and goes fast asleep like a baby. When I wakes up, I'm cured entirely."

"Duw Duw," said Mr Ifans, greatly impressed. "That sounds like a devil of a fine cure. Is your wife at home just now?"

Good Breeding in Ambleston

Early in the last century young Aby Wilkins from London was a member of the militia, and he was drafted to Pembrokeshire to sort out some trouble with the natives. While in the county he met and fell passionately in love with Martha, a young lady who lived on a small farm near Ambleston. He was assured that the feeling was mutual, and shortly afterwards came home to London on leave. He told his father that when he returned for another tour of duty to Pembrokeshire he would ask for her hand in marriage.

The astute father took Aby on one side for a bit of advice. "My boy," he said, "you must be very careful. I have your welfare at heart, and want you to make a good marriage. But you must be businesslike about these things. The girl's father must come down with something handsome. If he's an honest man he ought to put down £500. If he is a bankrupt, say £750. And if he is in prison, which we hope to God he is not, you should ask for £1000, no less."

A week later, Aby was sent back to Pembrokeshire with the militia. His father waited impatiently for some message concerning a marriage settlement, and after a few weeks a letter came by the Royal Mail. Inside the envelope was a simple message from Aby, which read:

"Dearest Papa, the father of my beloved and adorable Martha was hanged for sheep-stealing last Friday. What amount do you suggest?"

Life in the Hills

Ezra was a bachelor farmer who lived in the rough country up near Puncheston. He decided one day that if he did not get a move on he would be getting past his prime. Further, his smallholding was too small to make a decent living, and his life was blessed with very few luxuries. The rain was coming through the roof, and his old cart-horse had died. Ezra thought to himself that if he did not begin to woo and find himself a wife, the good things of life would quite pass him by.

He determined to offer himself to Bessie, a middle-aged widow who lived on the farm next door. She was a striking woman, and more to the point, she was known to have a few hundred pounds put away. Ezra wooed and won; the two farms were combined, and the estate began to take on an air of greater prosperity.

In due course Ezra decided that he needed to use some of his wife's wealth to replace his old cart-horse. So he bought a new one, and when he proudly led it into the yard he called his wife out of the kitchen. Bessie looked at the animal approvingly. "Ooh, that's a fine beast indeed," she said. "Well, Ezra, if it hadn't a bin for me silver, it wouldn't a bin here."

"Right you are, Bessie bach," replied Ezra. "If it hadn't a bin for yer silver you wouldn't a bin here yerself!"

A Quiet Celebration

Willy Parcel was new in Crymych, and had not learnt the essential details of local life. He was cycling down the farm lane towards the main road, having just delivered the mail to a lonely smallholding named Trefach. He was surprised to meet Abel the farmer coming the other way, looking very groggy indeed. "Good day to you, Abel Trefach, "said Willy. "There's smart you are. Sunday best, if I'm not mistaken. And fresh polish on your boots, indeed. Been out, have you? Funny time to be coming home, this time of the morning."

"Oh dear, there's rough I feel," replied Abel. "Been to Crymych, I have, celebrating my Golden Wedding. The boys led me astray. I missed the last bus home, so I slept in the hedge and walked all the way back."

"Your Golden Wedding?" queried Willy. But I just saw Maggie back at the farm, churning the butter."

"Don't be daft, Willy bach," said Abel. "She had got nothin' to do with it. It was the Golden Weddin' of me an' dear Liza, God rest her soul. Next week I celebrates the Silver Weddin' of me an' Bronwen, God rest her soul. That there Maggie have got a long way to go afore **she** does any celebratin'."

Another Point of View

Billy, Benny and Bobby were three old school friends who came from Narberth. As the years passed they went their separate ways, but they returned to Narberth every five years for a reunion. On one such occasion they were sitting in the bar of their favourite pub, catching up on each other's news. It transpired that Billy was still unmarried, that Benny's wife had just run off with the next door neighbour, and that Bobby was happy to be away from his wife for a few days. On hearing Benny's bad news, Billy Said: "Very sorry to hear of your trouble, old friend. It must be very hard to lose your wife." Benny smiled ruefully, but before he could say anything Bobby intervened. "Hard?" he said. "I should think so! As far as I can see it's almost impossible!"

The Opportunist from the Hills

Daniel Morgan came into a sum of money, sold his little farm near Maenclochog and bought a bigger farm in the lowlands near Wiston. He decided that he had better get to know the neighbours, so he called in to see the old man who ran the farm next door. He was delighted to find that he had a number of charming daughters, and met three of them over a cup of tea. When they had left the old man took his visitor to one side and said proudly: "I am very pleased to see the way my girls have turned out. I'd like to see them comfortably married, and since I have made a bob or two over the years they won't go penniless to their husbands. There is young Mary, only twenty years old, and a really good girl. I shall give her £250 when she marries. Then comes Bessie, who is twenty-five, and I'll giver her £500. And the man who takes dear Eliza, who is thirty, will find that she brings with her £750."

Daniel looked most impressed. He reflected for a moment and then said: "You haven't got one about forty, have you?"

Chapter Nine

SPORTING TALES

How To Keep Fit

Billy Brock from Llangwm was too fond of the cream cakes and bitter beer, and he had a problem with his weight. He went to the doctor, who advised him to do some jogging.

"Very good, doctor," said Billy. "But how much should I do?"

"Oh, about ten miles each day should be sufficient." replied the doctor. "Give me a ring in a week's time and tell me how you're getting on."

A week later the phone rang in the doctor's surgery. "Hello, doc," said Billy. "I'm gettin' on fine. I've done about seventy miles so far."

"Excellent," said the doctor. "Come in this afternoon and I'll give you a check to see how much weight you've lost."

"Oh, I can't do that," came the reply. "Can't get back in time - I've just reached Builth Wells."

Miracle on the Golf Course

Up in Heaven, a few years ago, it was all the rage to play golf. Jesus Christ and various of the Saints enjoyed a couple of games per week on the heavenly golf courses which were at their disposal. But Jesus and St Brynach got bored, and one day they decided to go down to earth for a game on a Welsh course. "I know just the place," said Brynach, and he led Jesus down to the Newport Golf Course, beneath the shadow of Carningli where he had spent many days in contemplation during his time on earth.

Before they started off on their first round Jesus said to Brynach: "We've played against other often enough in the past, old friend. So just to make things more interesting this time, I'll be Arnold Palmer and you can be Greg Norman. What do you think?" Brynach agreed, and off they went. After a while Jesus played a loose shot which sent the ball clean over the Nevern River to land on a mud bank on the other side. To play his next shot Jesus had to cross the river, and in order not to get his feet wet he walked on the water.

When Jesus was half-way across the river a couple of Newport golfers came by. One of them spotted Jesus and said to Brynach in amazement "Good God! Look at that! Who does he think he is? Jesus Christ?"

"Oh no," replied Brynach. "He thinks he's Arnold Palmer!"

A Considered Verdict

It was the occasion of the annual cricket match between Llangwm and Burton, and the two teams were fully dressed in their whites and rearing to go. At the last minute it was realised that one of the umpires was missing, and a stranger was persuaded to stand in his place. He was somewhat reluctant, but the players said to him "There's nothin' to it. You just looks carefully and if somethin' happens you just gives your honest opinion."

Llangwm went in to bat, and with the very first ball of the innings the opening batsman was tempted out of his crease and totally missed the ball. The wicket keeper did a brilliant bit of stumping. The Burton players leapt into the air, waved their arms about and cried with one voice "How's that?"

"Upon my soul," replied the temporary umpire. "I think it's marvellous!"

Hold-up in the Rough

Merfyn and Davy had never played golf before, but stimulated by the wonderful play of the Ryder Cup on the TV they decided that they would take up the game. The borrowed some clubs and balls, and turned up at Newport Golf Course for a round or two. All went well at first, but then the couple behind them on the fifth tee became very frustrated by the hold-up ahead of them. Davy was lying in the middle of the fairway having a snooze in the sun, and Merfyn was nowhere to be seen. Soon there were four couples waiting at the tee, and eventually one of the golfers strode down the course and confronted Davy. "Why don't you help your friend to find his ball?" he shouted.

"Oh, he've got his ball all right," replied Davy. "Down on the beach, he is, lookin' for his club."

A Sporting Chance

It is said that the men of Pembroke always have an eye open for the main chance. One day William, a young man from Pembroke, travelled by train to Tenby for a day at the seaside. He went for a long walk on the beach, and returned to the town along the edge of the golf course. It so happened that as he was passing by a golfer struck a particularly vigorous shot, which resulted in the ball striking William on the head. He fell to the ground, out for the count.

When he came to, he found that he was surrounded by concerned golfers, who insisted on carrying him into the club-house where he was administered a stiff drink. When he was fully recovered he said he must get going so as not to miss his train home, at which point the vigorous golfing gentleman pressed a pound note into his hand and bade him farewell. "Thank you very much, sir," said William. "An' when might you be playin' golf again?"

Where Did It Get Them?

Cuthbert Higgins was a recent convert to the game of golf, and enthused at great length about its beneficial impact upon body and soul. One day he was holding forth in the bar of the Tenby Golf Club. He said to anybody who cared to listen: "Golf is the most wonderful game ever invented. I tell you, boys, it will be the salvation of the nation. It sharpens up the mind. With healthy exercise it strengthens the body. If everybody in Britain played golf it would lengthen the life-span of every man, woman and child by at least a decade."

"But what about our ancestors?" asked the barman. "They never played golf, and they managed all right."

"But that's where you are wrong," replied Cuthbert. "These famous ancestors lived out their miserable lives in ignorance, unaware of the health-giving properties of the great game. And where are they now? Well, I'll tell you. Dead! All dead!"

Chapter Ten

PEMBROKESHIRE JUSTICE

The Perfect Witness

Tommy Williams of Neyland was up in court for heaving a brick through his neighbour's window during an argument about a racing pigeon. The only witness was a little girl who happened to be playing in the street at the time of the incident.

Before placing the child in the witness box the judge had to ascertain that she was capable of giving evidence and that she understood the nature of the oath.

"Now then, young lady," said the judge. "You must realise that this is a serious matter. When you give an oath you must tell the truth. Do you know what it means to swear an oath in court?"

"Yes sir," replied the little girl. "Damn and blast, you're a miserable old bugger. Is that all right. sir?"

When he had recovered his composure, the judge asked: "Do you know what will happen to you if you tell the court something that didn't happen?"

"Yes sir. I'll lose the quid what Tommy Williams promised me when a told me what to say."

Mitigating Circumstances

"Billy Jenkins," said the judge in a sober voice. "You have been found guilty of breaking and entering the business premises of Messrs Osborn and Perkins and stealing five Chelsea buns. It appears from the record that you have thirty-seven

previous convictions for petty theft, twenty-five convictions for breaking and entering, and eighteen convictions for assault and battery. Yours is a quite deplorable record. And what have you got to say for yourself? Are there any mitigating circumstances to which you wish to draw my attention before I sentence you?"

"Yes indeed, yer Honour," said Billy. "As the Good Lord said, nobody's perfect."

Dafydd Daft and the Jury

Dafydd Daft was always in trouble with the law, and he had been hauled up before the Eglwyswrw magistrates many times. This time he had gone too far, and his crime justified a trial before a judge and jury in the County Court. When the jury had been selected the judge looked at the downcast prisoner in the dock and said "Dafydd, it is now your privilege to challenge any member of the jury now being impanelled."
At this, Dafydd brightened considerably. "Thank you, your honour," he said. "I'll fight the small man with one eye over there at the end of the front row."

Dafydd Daft Helps Out

Dafydd was up before the Eglwyswrw magistrates again, this time for deserting his wife and children. After hearing all the facts of the case, and failing to hear of any mitigating circumstances from Dafydd or his solicitor, the magistrates went into recess. At last they returned, and the presiding magistrate said: "Mr Daft, this is a very serious matter, and there appears to be no excuse for your irresponsible behaviour. I therefore award your wife £500 a month."

"That is most kind of you indeed, your honour,"replied Dafydd. "In fact I'll try and give her a few quid myself."

Beautiful Justice in Newport Town

Once upon a time a Newport man was up before the Judge at the County Assizes for sheep stealing. At the end of the trial the Judge summoned the prisoner. "Dafydd ap Gwynn ap Ifan, stand up!" The prisoner stood in the dock.

"Dafydd ap Gwynn ap Ifan," said his honour, "in but a few short weeks it will be spring. The milky snows of winter will flee away, the emerald ice will vanish in the twinkling of an eye, and the air will become soft and balmy. In short, Dafydd ap Gwynn ap Ifan, the annual miracle of the year's re-awakening will occur.

"The gentle Afon Nyfer will run its whispering course to the sea. The timid snowdrops and cheerful primroses will show their tender blossoms to the world, and in the lanes of Cilgwyn the stately ash and ancient oak will put forth their fresh new shoots. The glorious flanks of Carningli will be ablaze with the golden gorse and the mighty peak will gaze down benignly upon the baronial domain of Cemais. From every tree-top some wild-wood songster will carol his mating song. Butterflies will sport in the sunshine and the busy bee will hum happily as it pursues its course from heather to bluebell. The gentle breezes will tease the tassels of the wild green grasses. And all of nature, Dafydd ap Gwynn ap Ifan, will be glad.

"But you, you miserable despicable little swine, won't be here to see any of it, for you will be hung up on the gallows at 10 o'clock on Tuesday morning."

A Simple Question

Silas Baker of Hakin had witnessed a traffic accident in Charles Street in Milford Haven, and had the misfortune to be called to the County Court to give evidence. He was called to the witness box, and in the course of a somewhat ponderous cross-examination the defending counsel said: "Now my good sir, we come to the crux of the matter. I want you to answer this question in as few words as possible, whether, when you were crossing the street, and the omnibus was coming down on the right side with the taxi opposite on the left and the motor-car trying to pass the bus, you saw the plaintiff between the two, or whether you saw him at all; whether he was near the taxi, the omnibus or the motor-car, or all of them or either, or which of them respectively?"

"You has got it exactly right," said Silas. "I couldn't have put it better meself."

A Man of Character

Winston Jones was up before the Pembroke Dock magistrates, but after the damning evidence was presented to the court the presiding magistrate thought that he should really hear something in the nature of a defence. "Have you anything to say in your defence?" he asked. "Only that I'm a man of exceedin' fine character," replied Winston.

"Well, is there anybody in court who can vouch for your good character?" asked the magistrate.

"Why yes, yer honour," said Winston. "That police sergeant over by there in the corner can vouch for me character."

"But your honour," blurted out the police sergeant, "I don't even know the man."

"Please observe, your worship," said Winston, triumphant, "I've lived all these years in Pembroke Dock an' the police sergeant don't even know me yet! How's that for bein' of good character?"

True Remorse

Iolo Dafis was up in court in Eglwyswrw for making a public nuisance of himself on New Year's Eve. The magistrate was not amused, and after hearing the evidence asked Iolo what he had to say in his defence.

"My lord, ladies and gentlemen of the jury, and officers of the law," said Iolo with a flourish, addressing an imaginary multitude and waving his arms in the air, "I have done a terrible crime, and very guilty I am indeed. All I can say, your esteemed Lordship, is that I shall be overburdened with remorse and seekin' for redemption until my dying day. That is, your Lordship, always assumin' that the Good Lord allows me to live that long."

Chapter Eleven

CARDI TALES

Give unto the Lord -- but not yet

Two old men belonged to the congregation of the Baptist Chapel in Cardigan. One Sunday morning they met after the morning service, and one said to the other: "Duw Duw, Albert, the state of the local economics is in good hands with the younger generation."

"Indeed? And what makes you say that, George?"

"Didn't you see young Morris Siop in chapel this morning? Sitting right behind him, I was. With his young son, he was. Just before the collection he pinched him, and when the boy cried he had to take him out. Saved him a couple of bob, that's for sure."

The Crafty Cardi

Once upon a time there was a wealthy farmer from Pembrokeshire who had three special friends. One of them came from Carmarthen; another from Haverfordwest; and the third from Cardigan. When the farmer died, his will stated that all his worldly possessions were to be shared equally between his three friends. But there were two conditions. Each friend had to be present at his funeral, and as a parting gesture each one had to place a gift of £100 in his cold hands as he lay in his open coffin before burial.

And so the morning of the funeral came. The three friends visited the farmer's house and, each in turn, they went into the room where the open coffin lay. The old farmer was laid out in style, dressed in his best suit and with a stiff starched collar. The Pembrokeshire man went in first, paid his last respects, and placed one hundred crisp pound notes in the dead man's hands. Then the Carmarthen man did the same. Finally Evans, the Cardigan man, went in. He took his wallet from his pocket, and discovered that it contained not even a halfpenny. He felt in his jacket pockets and trouser pockets, and fared no better. "Never

mind though," he said to himself. "The old man will not be without his due."

And he took a cheque book from his waistcoat and carefully wrote out a cheque for £300. Taking the two hundred pound notes from the coffin as change, he placed the cheque in the dead man's hand. Then he replaced the lid on the coffin and went out of the room with a clear conscience, a bulging wallet, and an angelic smile on his face.

The Even Craftier Cardi

Shortly after the visit of the Crafty Cardi to the room where the coffin lay, another gentleman came in. He had been asked by the deceased man's family to be one of the bearers at the funeral, and he also happened to come from Cardigan. Being a careful Cardi, he thought he'd better check that all was well in the coffin; and it occurred to him that he'd better have a quick rummage through the dead man's pockets just in case anything had been left there by accident.

On opening the coffin lid, the gentleman was greatly surprised to find a cheque in the dead man's hands. He prised it loose, opened it out, and was delighted to see the words "Pay the bearer £300", followed by the signature of one of the old farmer's friends.
"Duw Duw, there's nice of old Evans ," he said to himself. "Not often that

people recognises the value of a good bearer. This little piece of paper must be for me." Then he replaced the coffin lid, screwed it down tight, and said not a word to anybody.

On the day after the funeral he went to the bank in Cardigan and cashed the cheque. When he found out, old Evans was not amused, for instead of being £200 richer, he was now £100 poorer than he had been before the funeral.

Tragedy in Penparc

A tourist was speeding through Penparc on his way to Cardigan when he ran over Del Ifans' chicken and killed it stone dead. Stricken with remorse, the motorist picked up the dead bird and took it to the village shop, where he asked who the owner might be. "Oh yes, that will be belonging to Del Ifans," said the shopkeeper. So the motorist went to Del's house and admitted his crime.

"I am terribly sorry about your chicken, sir," said the tourist. "It ran out just in front of me and there was nothing I could do. If I give you £5 will that be all right?"

"Oh dear me." said Del, when he had recovered from the shock. "That was a very special hen. Better make it £10. You see, I has a cockerel that was very attached to that hen, and I am greatly afeared that when he finds out that she's dead the shock might kill him as well."

Using the System

Two penniless men met in Haverfordwest. One of them was a farmer from Cardigan, and the other was a Scot from Aberdeen. Both were in Pembrokeshire in the hope of finding jobs on the oil rigs. They were both thirsty and miserable, but then the Scot had an idea for getting a free drink. "There is a barmaid in the Milford Arms who likes to be chatted up a bit," he said. "She also has a bad memory, and after a while she can't remember whether you've paid or not. Let's see if we can pull it off. I'll try first."

So they went into the Milford Arms, and the Cardi sat in the corner while the Scot duly got his free drink. Now it was the Cardi's turn to try, and he went up to the bar to order his pint. Soon he was engaged in deep conversation, telling the girl all about life in Cardiganshire. After ten minutes of animated discussion, he drained his glass and said: "Well, it's been nice talking to you, Susan. But now I must be off to meet a business colleague. What about my change?"

The Cardigan Death Test

Jeremiah Pugh was a respected councillor in Cardigan. He fell ill, and one evening a new GP from the local Health Centre received a call from his wife. "Please to call round, doctor bach," she said. "I think my beloved Jeremiah has just departed this life."

The doctor arrived within a few minutes, and started an examination of the body. "What are you doing, doctor bach?" asked Mrs Pugh. "Well now," replied the new GP, "I have to carry out these little tests just to make sure that your dear husband really has passed away."

"Oh, you needn't bother with all that," said the grieving wife. You're new around these parts, I suppose. All you need is a silver half-crown."

"And what on earth would I do with a silver half-crown, Mrs Pugh?"

"Just put in in the palm of his right hand, doctor bach. If his fingers don't close up to grasp it within a minute, the Good Lord have surely took him to Himself. We do say in Cardigan town that when the right hand have gone, bein' the money hand, there's no more point in stayin' alive anyway."

Not So Urgent

Early one morning Dr Jones of Cardigan was sound asleep after an all-night case when he was awakened by the incessant ringing of his telephone. He dragged himself wearily to the phone and picked up the receiver. "Doctor, Doctor," said a female voice at the other end, "this is Thomas Brynawelon. Please come at once! A matter of life and death it is!" And with that the line went dead. The good doctor dressed hurriedly and rushed out of the house.

When he arrived at Brynawelon he found that the caller and her family were all perfectly calm. "It's all right now, doctor bach," said Mrs Thomas. "You could just as well have stayed at home."

The doctor was furious. "Then why did you call me out?" he demanded.

"Well now, doctor," interjected the man of the house. "Little Billy told us he'd swallowed a half-crown, and we feared the worst. Things was looking very bad indeed. But then we realised it was only a penny piece he'd swallowed. We found the half-crown on the floor and then we felt much better."

The Cardi Visitor

Caleb Owen of Cardigan went off to visit his cousin in Cardiff. He had a wonderful time, for Cousin George treated him remarkably well. He drank well, ate well, was taken round to see the sights of the city, and even got a free ticket to a rugby international at the Arms Park. He overstayed his welcome by a week, and at last realised that his host was getting weary of his company. When George had taken him to the right platform on Cardiff station for the journey home, he said: "Cousin George bach, there's good you have been to me. I have ate well and drank well, and the match was wonderful, indeed I don't know how to thank you, but I'll send you a hen now then, when I get home."

"Why, that's most kind of you, Caleb," said George. "I shall look forward to that." And he waved him goodbye.

About a year later the two cousins met up again at a family funeral. "Good day, Caleb," said George. "I thought you were going to send me a hen?"

"So I was, Cousin George bach," replied Caleb. "But it never died."

The Crafty Cardi Goes to Town

A wealthy Cardigan merchant was travelling to London by train in the first class compartment. At first he was alone in the carriage, but at Whitland a Pembrokeshire man got in, and later another businessman joined them at Carmarthen station. As the journey went on the three got to talking about their great wealth and successful businesses. The conversation lapsed, and the three men settled into reading their newspapers. Then, as if to reinforce his boasts, the Pembrokeshire man put down his copy of "The News Chronicle". He ostentatiously took out a cigarette, lifted a pound note out of his wallet, ignited it with a match, and then lit his cigarette with it. A little later, not to be out-done, the Carmarthenshire man set aside his copy of "The Times". He extracted a splendid cigar from his gold cigar case, took out a five pound note, set it alight with a match, and applied it to his cigar.

A long time passed, with the three passengers apparently engrossed in their newspapers. Nobody said a word. At last the Cardiganshire man put down his newspaper. He rummaged in his pocket and took out a long briar pipe. Then, with no great haste packed it carefully with the finest tobacco. This task having been completed, and with his two travelling companions peeping over the tops of their newspapers, he slowly reached into his inside pocket. He took out his cheque book and, very deliberately, wrote out a cheque, saying quietly to himself "Pay the bearer one hundred pounds." Then he slowly put away the cheque book, put a match to the cheque, and used it to light his pipe. That having been done, he puffed away contentedly in a cloud of smoke all the way to London, totally absorbed in his copy of "The Tivyside Advertiser".

Griff and the Match

Griff Morgan was a Cardigan man who travelled quite frequently on the "Cardi Bach" train between Cardigan and Whitland. One day he was settled happily into his corner seat, smoking his pipe as the train puffed its way towards Crymych. He got into conversation with a fellow passenger, and in due course the stranger took out his own pipe and started to fumble about in his pockets. Clearly he was searching for something.

"Dear me," he exclaimed, "I appear to have come out today without my matches. Can you oblige?"

Griff took a match out of his matchbox and handed it over. The fumbling continued, with the stranger making a great show of hunting through his pockets one by one. While all this was going on, Griff continued to smoke his pipe contentedly. At last the stranger spoke again.

"This is really most annoying," he said. "I seem to have left my tobacco at home."

"Ah well," replied Griff. "You'd better be givin' me the match back, as you'll not be havin' any use for it now."

Flexible Response

A benevolent old lady was walking past the Guildhall in Cardigan when she observed a beggar sitting on the steps with a sign next to him which said "Lame - local man, wife and six children to support." She stopped and looked with compassion on the poor man, and then placed a penny in his outstretched hand. "My poor fellow," she said, "here is a coin for you. Goodness me, it must be terrible to be lame. But I think it would be even worse to be blind." "Yer right, lady," agreed the beggar. "When I was blind I was always gettin' buttons and juke box tokens!"

A Stout Defence

A Cardigan man was travelling on the road to Narberth when he was leapt upon by three highwaymen. He put up a ferocious struggle but at long last the villains managed to pin him to the ground. On going through his pockets they found nothing but a bent six-penny piece. Surprised that the man had put up such a struggle in defence of such a small coin, one highwayman said to the others: "A must be a Cardi. And if a'd had a shillin' piece in 'is pocket a'd have surely killed the three of us!"

Helping the War Effort

In the Second World War the good people of Cardigan were encouraged - like other citizens throughout the land - to put their money into War Savings. One day as Dai was coming out of the Post Office he met the local minister. "Good day to you, Dai," said the reverend gentleman. "I see you have been laying up treasure on earth, and at the same time helping the war effort."

"No, no, reverend bach," replied Dai. "I always comes into the Post Office on a Thursday to fill up me fountain pen."

Davy's Treasure

Davy Diamond was a labourer with a Cardigan building firm. He went up to Cardiff with the local rugby club to watch the Wales-England international match, and while he was there he did a bit of shopping. When he came back he showed all his friends at work a fine pair of gold cufflinks with large "diamonds" mounted on them. He wore them with pride every Sunday to chapel, and they were looked on with envy by family and friends. He treated with contempt any suggestion that they were not made with 18 carat gold and authentic diamonds. At last the foreman on the building site asked Davy, in strictest confidence, if the cuff-links from Cardiff had real diamonds on them.

"Course they have!" said Davy. "And if they ain't real diamonds some blighter have done me out of two bob!"

No Liver Today

A Cardigan gentleman used to spend a penny a day on liver for his cat. One day he popped his head round the door of the butcher's shop and said:

"Don't you bother to send the liver round today, Billy. The cat have caught a mouse."

A Ha'penny for Luck

Tomos, a young man from Cardigan, well brought up and thrifty with it, was intent upon making his way in the world. He applied for a job in London, and was invited for an interview. He became very apprehensive at the prospect of such a long journey, for he had not previously been further afield than Carmarthen. On confessing his fears to a friend, the friend said: "Don't worry. I heard from an old gypsy once that on a long journey by train you will get good luck if you throw a halfpenny out of the window every time you cross a river on the way."

Encouraged by this, Tomos went off to London, first on the Cardi Bach through Crymych and then on the GWR to London. When he returned he met his friend in the street, and was asked how he had got on with the good luck recipe.

"Not too bad indeed," replied the traveller. "I got on well enough crossing the Towy in Carmarthen and the Loughor at Neath, but when I got to the Usk at Newport the string got caffled up in the girders of the bridge, and I lost my ha'penny."

The Religious Cardi

Mr Jones Generous was a religious Cardi gentleman who liked to watch his pennies, and think beautiful thoughts. One Sunday morning in chapel singing rousing hymns, he carelessly put a half crown on the collection plate, thinking it was a penny. Too late, he realised his mistake as the surprised sidesman nodded his approval and smiled a beatific smile. After that, the old gentleman only pretended to put money on the collection plate for the next thirty Sundays, till he was quits with God. From then on he examined his pennies very carefully before giving them to the Lord.

After some years Mr Jones stopped going to chapel because he was asked, once too often. to contribute to the Missionary Society. For the last twenty years of his life he made it his habit to listen to the Sunday morning service on the radio. He would settle down in his armchair and turn up the volume. He would sing lustily during the hymns and close his eyes devoutly during the prayers. When the collection was announced he would turn off the radio, and after a suitable time had elapsed he would turn it on again to continue with his devotions.

When at last he died the minister announced to the congregation: "Dear brothers and sisters, you will be moved to hear of the death of Mr Jones. His generosity was legendary. The funeral will be held in the chapel at 10 o'clock on Tuesday. I shall make a funeral address for the occasion, and the man himself will be here, for the first time in twenty years."

The Missing Threepenny Piece

A Cardigan man was once seen in a local hostelry, frantically turning out his pockets and with a distraught expression on his face. "What's the trouble, Sion?" asked a friend.

"I've lost a threepenny bit and I've searched every pocket but one."

"Why don't you look in the last pocket, then?" he was asked.

"I'm scared to death, man," replied Sion. "For if it's not there the shock will surely be the finish of me!"

Cardi Epistle

Letter from a Cardi written during a visit to London:

"Dear Mam, There's a grand time I'm having here. The restaurants are especial good, and if I sits at a table where somebody have just finished I often finds a couple of bob under the plate! Mind you keep my cold rice pudding from Sunday. See you Friday off the Cardi Bach.

PS If there is no stamp on the envelope it have fell off in the post."

Chapter Twelve

TRAVELLER'S TALES

Nasty Shock in Llangwm

The first time Green's Motors sent a double decker bus to Llangwm it was the cause of great excitement. Two elderly ladies decided that they would travel to Harfat to do their shopping in the new-fangled machine. Leaving their shopping baskets on the lower deck, they climbed upstairs and settled down in the front seat, full of eager anticipation of the journey ahead.

Suddenly, as the bus started to move, one of the old ladies let out a scream. "Blessed Lord, this is terrible!" she shouted to her friend Daisy. "We must get off quick. They've forgot to put a driver up here!"

Strange Experience in America

Kenny and Bob were from Milford, and for a long time they saved up for a package-deal holiday in New York. Shortly after they arrived they saw a stall on the street with a big sign above it that read "Hot Dogs -- One Dollar."

"Look at that!" said Kenny. "They eats dogs in this country. Well I never."

"Not a bad price," said Bob. "Try anything once. Shall we try one each?"

So the lads each bought a hot dog, and Bob started to tuck in. But then Kenny observed the long thin droopy sausage beneath the mustard and the tomato ketchup. "Not sure I likes the look of the bit I've got," he said. "I think I'll try the bitch next time. Which part of the bloody dog did you get?"

Hindrance near Camrose

Jack Wells Fargo had a donkey cart in Haverfordwest, which he used to carry small loads around the town. Sometimes he would collect parcels from the railway station destined for the local shops, and on other occasions he would transport (very slowly) horse manure, potatoes, sand and gravel, and all manner of other useful things.

One day, after a very stormy night, he had to deliver a load to a remote farm near Camrose, and found that a large branch had fallen across the road. The way was not quite barred, but the branch was just too low for his donkey to pass beneath.

So Jack went to a nearby farm, borrowed a pick and shovel, and started to dig a hole in the road beneath the fallen branch. While he was at work a passing tramp asked him what he was doing. "Tryin' to get me donkey an' cart through on me urgent mission to Camrose," said Jack.

"Well," said the tramp, "if it's the branch that's the trouble, why don't yer simply move it away?"

"Don't be daft," replied Jack. "Anybody can see it's the road that's the problem. If only it were twelve inches lower down there wouldn't have bin no hindrance in the first place." And with that he carried on with his digging.

Sin in Maenclochog

An Englishman was on holiday in Maenclochog. He thought it rather quiet, and asked in the local pub one evening where all the action was. "There is quite enough action for us, boyo," said Dai from behind the bar. "You should see this place on a Saturday night!"

"That may well be," said the Englishman. "But what about the women? Where are all the women? There must be some, for goodness sake, who are after a bit of fun in this God-forsaken hole."

Gwilym was in on the conversation, and he told the Englishman to come and have a quiet word in the corner. Once they were out of earshot of the others, Gwilym whispered conspiratorially: "It's a terrible thing, man, but the chapel people have driven all the loose women out of town. Beloved Blodwen and one or two of the other girls can be found down in the cave every night around 9 o'clock. Go down across Willy Evans's field -- no torches, mind -- and you will see the entrance to the cave. Shout yoo-hoo-hoo outside the cave. If there is no reply that means the girls is all busy, but if you hears yoo-hoo-hoo coming back, you can go in and negotiate."

The Englishman was most excited at this news, and later that evening he made his way across the muddy field in the pitch darkness. He got in a terrible mess, but he was inflamed by passion, and would not be deterred from his mission. At last he was able to make out the entrance of the cave below him in a hollow, and shouted "Yoo-hoo-hoo!"

There was no reply, and so he waited. Then it came on to rain, and the poor fellow got soaked to the skin. He shouted yoo-hoo-hoo many times, but there was never any reply. At last, thoroughly fed up, he shouted "Yoo-hoo-hoo" at the top of his voice, intending to go back to the village immediately afterwards; and he was amazed and delighted when the reply "Yoo-hoo-hoo! Yoo-hooooooo!" came from the cave.

Full of excitement, the Englishman scrambled down the slope in the pouring rain and rushed into the dark entrance of the cave, where he was run over by the 10 o'clock goods train from Rosebush.

Engine Trouble

In the early days of passenger flights, Iolo and Islwyn from Maenclochog were in a posh four-engined aeroplane en route from Dublin to Cardiff. They were looking down on their home territory of Pembrokeshire from a great height when they heard the captain's voice over the loudspeaker. "Ladies and gentlemen," he said. "I am sorry to have to tell you that engine number one has just failed. There is nothing to worry about, but we will be fifteen minutes late arriving in Cardiff."

Five minutes later, the captain's voice was heard again. "Ladies and gentlemen," he said. "Engine number two has just packed up. Everything is quite safe, but we will now be thirty minutes late arriving in Cardiff." A minute later there came another announcement: "Sorry about this, ladies and gentlemen, but engine number three has just caught fire. The plane flies very well on one engine, but unfortunately we will now be sixty minutes late with our arrival."

"Good gracious me," said Iolo to his companion. "Do you realise that if number four engine fails we'll be up here all night?"

Avoiding Action

Eddie and Bert had just been finishing the harvest in a big field near Narberth, and were driving the combine harvester down a narrow lane on the way back to the farmyard. Suddenly an English holidaymaker came round the bend in a very fast Mercedes, and when confronted by the combine harvester filling the whole of the road he had to take drastic avoiding action. The car went up onto the hedge, did two somersaults in mid-air, and landed on its roof in the field. The tourist and his wife staggered out of the vehicle looking distinctly groggy.

Bert turned to Eddie and said "Good Lord! Did you see that?"

"Indeed I did," replied Eddie. "The Gods is with us today, that's for sure. We just got out of that field in time."

On the Wrong Bus

A prominent minister from Tenby was travelling home one night on a Silcox bus from a prayer meeting in Saundersfoot. As the bus rocked along the narrow road he was greatly annoyed by a young man who got on at New Hedges and sat down next to him. He was much the worse for drink, and insisted on singing at the top of his voice.

At last the minister could contain himself no longer, and said to the youth: "Young man, do you realise that you are on the road to perdition and damnation?"

"Oh Hell," replied the young man. "I could have sworn this was the bus to Penally and Manorbier."

Sam's Intrepid Voyage

Once upon a time there was a Llangwm lad who was none too bright. He was seventeen years old and had lived a sheltered life, never having travelled further afield than Hook. He decided that he would travel to Haverfordwest to experience the delights of the big city, and accordingly he discussed his plans with his friend Bert. "Tha can go up the river," said Bert. "It'll only take thee two hours if that keeps rowin', but tha must stick to a nice steady rhythm, like. Take thy pocket watch with thee and tha'll know when tha's got there."

So Sam decided he would steal a rowing boat from a mooring in Black Tar. He waited for a pitch-black night, and crept out of his house having packed up a little bag. He went through the sleeping village, stole a boat from Black Tar, and set off up the river. He rowed furiously for two hours in the darkness, quite unaware that there was a strong ebb tide flowing and that his boat was making no progress whatsoever. Eventually, in the first light of dawn, he heard a voice from the shore, which shouted: "Is that you, Sam? What's tha doin' out there paddlin' away in the middle of the river?" "Well, I'll be damned," said Sam to himself, still not lifting his eyes from the bottom of the boat, "who can it be that knows me all the way up here in Harfat?"

Trouble on the Railway

The Great Western Railway was being built on the outskirts of Haverfordwest, and hundreds of Irish navvies were billeted in the town. Almost every night there was trouble in the public houses of Prendergast, and free-for-all fist fights were particularly common on pay-days when there was ready cash about and when the ale flowed freely. One day a group of battered navvies, swathed in bandages and hobbling on crutches, were brought before the local magistrate. Seamus O'Malley was asked by the magistrate to describe the circumstances of the fight which had occurred in "The Bull" on the previous Friday night.

"Well, yer Honour," replied Seamus. "Billy Murphy got in a bit of an argument wid Pat Dooley. Pat smashed Billy over the head wid a chair and busted his head open. Then Billy's brother Mike carved Pat up wid a butcher's knife, and Barry Flanagan got a shot-gun and shot Mike through the leg. Charlie Casey went at Barney wid an axe, an' then, yer Honour, we jus' naturally got to fightin'."

Professional Advice

In the 1950s the Fishguard-Rosslare passenger route was served by an old steamship called the "Innisfallen". A new clerk had started work in the booking office, and he had been carefully briefed by his boss to be as helpful as possible to those purchasing tickets. One day there was a long queue at the ticket window, but the gentleman at the head of the queue was unfamiliar with the niceties of sea travel.

"Upper or lower berth?" asked the clerk.

"What's the difference?"

"Well, the difference is five shillings. The lower berth is higher than the upper one. The higher price is for the lower. If you want it lower you will have to go higher. We sell the upper lower than the lower. Most people don't like the lower upper, although it's lower on account of being higher. When you occupy an upper you have to go up to lie down and get down to get up, and the advantage with the lower is that you only have to go down to lie down and go up to get up. So you will appreciate, sir, why the higher berth is lower and the lower berth is higher."

Strange Passenger in Crymych

There was a big funeral going on in one of the chapels in Crymych. During the service a row of vehicles, including the hearse, was parked on the street outside. After the service the coffin was placed in the hearse and the chief mourners climbed into the cars for the journey to the Narberth Crematorium. One of the mourners, an old college friend of the deceased, was surprised to find a stranger in his car, but he assumed he was one of the funeral party and said nothing at first.

After five minutes, with the convoy making steady progress along the Narberth road, the driver said: "You'll be a brother of the corpse then?"

"No," replied the stranger.

After another five minutes the driver tried again to open a conversation:

"Maybe you'll be a cousin of the corpse?"

"No", came the answer.

"Is it a friend of the corpse, then?"

"No indeed," said the passenger, emphatically. "Evans Tybach was a miserable old sod, and owed me a thing or two. I has to get some chicken feed, and thought I'd just have a little lift with the funeral as far as the Clynderwen Co-op!"

Tragedy in Clarbeston Road

An old farmer who lived near Clarbeston Road had a fine herd of milking cows. His land was bisected by the GWR railway line, and when the fields on the far side of it were being grazed he had to drive his cows across the line four times a day - twice over and twice back - for milking. One day there was a sad accident, and his best cow, whose name was Margaret, was struck by a train on the level crossing and killed. He complained to the GWR and was sent a claim form to fill in. For hours he struggled with question after question, filling in the answers as best he could. Then he came to the last item, which read "Disposition of the carcass?" He puzzled over this for a very long time, chewing the end of his pencil. At last he wrote, quite truthfully: "Kind and gentle".

Good Service on the Sleeper

In the good old days there was an overnight GWR sleeper train between Paddington and Milford Haven. "Now then," said a passenger as he climbed aboard at the London end, "I must get off the train when we arrive at Whitland. Will you kindly wake me and put me off there?"

"Yes indeed, sir," replied the guard. "It will be my pleasure." And he received a handsome tip, in advance, from the passenger.

"And by the way," added the gentleman, "don't be too upset if I protest a bit when you come to shake me. I'm a heavy sleeper and take a while to wake up properly. Just put me out on the platform, even if I have a bit of a temper."

In the morning he awoke and discovered that the train was long past Whitland, and indeed was just arriving in Milford Haven. He was furious, and after finding the guard he told him off in no uncertain fashion.

"Oh dear!" said the guard. "I thought you was in compartment number five. I sees now that you do have a bit of a temper, sir, but it's nothin' compared to the temper of the gentleman I put out at Whitland!"

A Chance Meeting

Myfanwy Evans had been up to London on a Richards Brothers coach trip, to visit the Flower Show and do a bit of shopping. She met her friend Mary down by the post office in St Dogmaels.

"Well, Mary bach," she said. "There's a wonderful time I had in the big city. And the crowds! Never seen anything like it, not even in Cardigan on Barley Saturday."

"There's nice," said Mary.

"And guess what?" continued Myfanwy. "You'll never guess who I saw in London on Thursday morning."

"Who was that then? Go on, tell me."

"I saw Billy Williams."

"No! Not cousin Billy Williams from Boncath?"

"Yes indeed. The very same. Cousin Billy from Boncath."

"Where did you see him? I never knew he was in London."

"In Oxford Street, it was. I saw him looking into the shop window of Littlewoods. Looking at some tailor's dummies in bikinis he was. And do you know what, Mary bach?"

"No. Tell me what happened, then."

"I was so pleased to see him," said Myfanwy, blushing, "that I went up behind him and gave him a big hug and a big kiss on his cheek, just to give him a nice little surprise. And do you know what, Mary bach? There's ashamed I was, for it wasn't him at all!"

The Trouble with London

Albert was an ancient resident of Johnston. Ever since anyone could remember he had occupied the same settee by the fireplace in the public bar of the local hostelry. He came in every night at 8 o'clock and left at 10 o'clock, having drunk two pints of bitter. It was well known that he had never been further afield than Carmarthen. One day somebody discovered that Albert was shortly due to celebrate his ninetieth birthday, and the regulars organized a whip-round for him. They raised enough money for a tidy present, and the landlord suggested that they should buy him a Weekend Mini-holiday in London. Albert was pressed - somewhat reluctantly - into accepting the gift, and on Friday morning the landlord and a few friends waved him off from Johnston railway station.

On Monday night he was back in the pub in his usual seat by the fire, obviously none the worse for his adventure.

"So how was it, Albert?" asked one of the regulars. "What did you think of the big wicked city?"

"Oh, it was grand," replied Albert. "The people! You have never seen such crowds, boys. And the clothes! Wonderful the way them maids wear skirts so short you can almost see their navels. And the buildings! So tall that they blots out the sky, and all made with great sheets of glass and shiny metal and gleaming white concrete. And the traffic! Never seen so many cars since I went to the County Show in 1952...."

And so he went on, regaling his listeners with graphic descriptions of the wonders of the capital of the realm. "Almost too much, it was," he concluded. Mind you, boys, I wouldn't mind goin' again some day afore I gets too old." Then a shadow came over his face, and there was a long pause before he said: "Tell you what, though. There's one thing that's very bad indeed about London."

"Oh, what's that then? Tell us, Albert."

"It's just that the place is so blinkin' **far** from everywhere."

Making Sure

The ferryboat was well on its way from Caldey Island to the mainland when a sudden storm blew up. The passengers became quite apprehensive, and their worries were not entirely removed when the ferryman, after a consultation with his mate, remarked: "If you don't mind, ladies and gents, we'll take yer tuppences now, for there's no knowin' what might come over us afore we reaches Tenby!"

The Educated Tramp

In the 1940s and 1950s an educated tramp named Alexander travelled widely throughout Pembrokeshire. Every year, in the month of June and regular as clockwork, he arrived in the parish of Rudbaxton and obtained some meagre food supplies from the local farmers' wives. They enjoyed chatting to him, for he had a civilized manner and knew a great deal more about the state of the world than they did.

One day Alexander knocked on a familiar back door but found that it was opened by a new owner, a lady new to the district. Alexander asked if he might, as usual, sleep in the barn for the night and if he might have a slice of bread and cheese and a cup of tea; but the lady refused, and rebuked him sharply for his decadent and unproductive life-style. She asked what had brought him to his present state.

"Well, it was like this," replied Alexander. "I was once a successful businessman, but I was just like you, madam, distributing vast sums to the poor and needy."

"That's all very well," said the lady. "But you should settle down and get back to work. Don't you know that a rolling stone gathers no moss?"

"Madam," said Alexander, "without evading your question, may I ask of what practical use moss would be to a man in my condition?"

Travelling in Style

The GWR train was chugging along merrily on its way from Haverfordwest to Paddington. One of the passengers in a first class compartment looked somewhat out of place among the smartly-dressed gentlemen who made the journey every week; and when the ticket collector came round the gentlemen awaited developments with interest.

On being asked for his ticket Billy (who was obviously a son of the soil) made a great show of not being able to find it. He searched in his trouser pockets, then in his jacket pockets, and then in his shopping bag, making the ticket collector more and more irritated. At last the exasperated official said: "Sir, you have had your ticket in your mouth all the time!" And with that he pulled it out, left the compartment and slammed the door.

A little later, when the coast was clear, Billy gave his fellow passengers a broad wink. "I ain't so daft as I looks," he said. "That was an ol' ticket I borrowed from me dad. I was just suckin' off the class an' the date, like, so as to keep the ticket collector happy."

The Weight of Years

Georgie and Gertie were getting on a bit. but they lived life to the full. They enjoyed driving around Pembrokeshire, and went out every Sunday from their comfortable home in Tenby for a visit to Bosherston Pools, Manorbier, Freshwater West or some other beauty-spot. One day, when they reached a beautiful viewpoint in the Gwaun Valley Gertie got out of the car and said: "Georgie, why don't you help me out of the car? You're not so gallant as you used to be when I was a gal."

"No indeed," retorted Georgie. "And you're not so buoyant as you used to be when I was a boy."

Message from India

In Manordeifi Church, close to the banks of the River Teifi near Llechryd, there is a memorial to a young British army soldier who died on active duty in India under mysterious circumstances. The story goes that in due course the Army shipped back a large and oddly-shaped box for burial. It didn't smell too good when it arrived at Llechryd, and on opening it up the soldier's family discovered an extremely large and partly decomposed tiger inside. A telegraph signal was sent off to India to ask whether some mistake had been made, and to insist that the body of the young man should be returned to the family post haste. Back came the reply from foreign parts, short and to the point: "Tiger in box. Sahib in tiger."

Two Travelling Men

Bert and Davy were commercial travellers, both covering West Wales and both selling cigarettes and confectionery to local tobacconists and sweet shops. They were deadly rivals, each one competing the whole time for an expansion of his market at the expense of the other. One day they met on the forecourt of the petrol station in Johnston, and the following conversation ensued.

"Morning, Bert."

"Morning, Davy. Where are you going?"

"Oh, just over to Neyland."

"You're telling me you're going to Neyland so that I'll think you're going to Milford Haven. But I'm not stupid. I happen to know from Williams Woodbine that you are in fact going to Neyland, so there is absolutely no point in telling me the truth."

A Helping Hand

A young man called Osmond, from Clarbeston Road, was travelling home by train from Swansea. When the ticket collector came round he asked Osmond where he was getting off. "Clarbeston Road," replied Osmond.

"Oh dear, that's impossible," said the ticket collector. "This train doesn't stop at Clarbeston Road on Tuesdays."

"Damn and blast," said Osmond. "Look, my old mother is ill, and it is absolutely vital that I get off at my home station today for humanitarian reasons."

"I'm very sorry indeed, sir, but I cannot break the regulations."

"Look," said Osmond, "this is really a matter of life and death. Here's a £20 note for you if you just ask the driver to slow down a bit so that I can jump off when we are going through the station."

So the ticket collector agreed, while warning Osmond to run like mad after his feet touched the ground so as to avoid serious injury. Sure enough, when the train reached Clarbeston Road station it slowed to a crawl, and Osmond jumped off and ran furiously along the platform as instructed. He was now travelling almost as fast as the train, and suddenly a hand shot out, grabbed him and dragged him on board. He was greeted by a smiling dining car attendant who said: "Thank goodness I was here to help you, sir. You are lucky to have got on board, because we don't stop at Clarbeston Road on Tuesdays."

The Wrong Jones

At the height of the Cold War a Russian spy was parachuted at dead of night into the wild country near Mynachlogddu, with the purpose of gathering information about the US Naval Facility at Brawdy. He had instructions to contact Mr Jones of Maenclochog. After a long walk he arrived in the village early in the morning and went to the Post Office, where he ascertained that a Mr Jones lived just up the road. He knocked on the appropriate door, which was duly opened by a gentleman. "Are you Mr Jones?" asked the spy. "Yes, I am," replied the man.

The spy looked furtively over his shoulder and said: "The tulips are blooming well today." "I beg your pardon?" "The tulips are blooming well today."

At last Mr Jones got the message. "My dear fellow, you have come to the wrong house," he said. "I am Jones Pentagon. You want Jones Kremlin, who lives at number fifteen."

How Things Change

Two teenagers from Pembrokeshire were standing on the platform at Paddington station, waiting for the train to take them home. They were in earnest conversation, and an elderly military gentleman standing nearby could not help but overhear them.

"Excuse me, gentlemen," he said to them. "I'm sure I recognise from your accent that you come from Pembrokeshire. I have many happy memories from my time there during the war. Tell me, do they still say "Why aye boy" in your part of the world?" At this, one of the lads immediately replied "Why no boy."

The Limits of Technology

Fred was walking up Prendergast Hill in Honey Harfat when he was met by his friend Sam. "Mornin' Fred," said Sam. "Wasn't that you I saw runnin' full pelt down the hill half an hour ago?"

"Indeed it was," replied Fred. "I was chasin' after some bugger what stole my old Austin Seven."

"But why were you runnin' after'n? Surely a could drive the car far faster'n you could run?"

"Oh yes," said Fred. "Goes like the wind it does. But I only puts in a pint o' petrol at a time, what with the terrible price it is. I reckoned the thief'd get about as far as Cartlett lime kills afore the engine packed up. Sure enough, I found'n in front of Green's Motors with his head under the bonnet. Now a's off to the police station with Constable Morris, an' I'm off home for another tumbler o' petrol to get the car goin' again."

Chapter Thirteen

IN TIMES OF SORROW

A Sorrowful Occasion

There was a big funeral going on in Prendergast Church in Haverfordwest. After the church service the undertaker was marshalling all the mourners into a procession for the short journey to the graveyard. He noticed a man standing a little apart from all the other mourners, looking very disconsolate. "Good morning, sir," said the undertaker. "Would you care to step this way and join the procession? I assume that you must be one of the mourners?"

"You bet I am!" replied the miserable man. "I lent the deceased ten quid and I've nothing to prove it!"

Not Much of a Life

Evan Jones and his wife Maisie lived in a little cottage called Penmynydd, not far from Puncheston. They had no children, but seemed contented enough in their old age. One dark winter's day, as is the way of the world, Mr Jones died. A few weeks later two local ladies met outside Puncheston Post Office. Their conversation went as follows:

"I sees in "The Telegraph" that poor old Jones Penmynydd died intestate."

"Oooh, there's a pity. That explains why they never had no children."

"Couldn't have been much fun for Mrs Jones bach, neither. All them years without the nuptuals. I wonder when he had the op?"

Generally Speaking

A visitor to the village of Manorbier was having a walk across the valley, and arrived at last in the churchyard. There he found the local grave-digger hard at work on a new grave, ready for a burial to take place on the following day. Keen to strike up a conversation, the visitor said. "Good afternoon, sir. What a very pleasant day it is. Tell me, do people round here die very often?"

There was a long silence, and then the sexton replied. "Well sir, I cannot say what happens over Lydstep way, and I hears that there is funny goin's on over by Jameston and Hodgeston, but generally speakin', in Manorbier itself, so far as I can make out, they tends to die just the once."

Comfort in Distress

A well-known character from Crymych died, having struggled for many years to make a success of his little farm in the misty hills. At the funeral his wife Mary wept and showed great grief, calling out at the grave side that all she wished was to lie in the grave with deceased. She was restrained from jumping in, and when the last sod was planted the mourners retired to the inn which stood near the graveyard. The usual comforts were resorted to by the chief mourners. One neighbour paid special attention to the widow; and after plying her with a few drinks he took his courage in both hands and said:

"Now then, Mary bach, there's no use breakin' your heart for poor Gwynfor that's gone. The likes of him was not within the four walls of the world, but I have been thinkin' of how he could to some extent be replaced to you, indeed, by offerin' myself, joinin' our bits of ground together, and what with the litter of pigs and the few pounds I have in the heel of my old stocking it all might to some extent make up for the sad bereavement that you have suffered."

Exhausted by this impressive speech. Tom stepped back and waited for a response. Mary wiped her eyes and with bent head and swaying body mournfully replied:

"There's grateful I am Tom, to be sure, for the kind words and tender thoughts you have given to the poor broken-hearted widow in her grief on this dark day; but I am sorry you spoke too late, for Billy Jenkins offered me the same consolation at the wake last night, and there, in the presence of the corpse, it would not have been right to refuse him."

The Smell of Welsh Cakes

Harold and Mabel lived in a little cottage on one of the back streets of Narberth. The cottage was immaculate, for Mabel was a fierce and tidy woman who liked to see everything in its place. She worked to a strict daily schedule, and was considerably inconvenienced when her husband fell ill and looked as if he might die. One day, after a visit from the doctor confirmed that he had not long to live, Mabel had to go shopping. "Harold," she said. "I won't be gone long. I has to get some flour and some raisins. But if you feels like dying afore I comes back, mind to blow out the candle first."

Harold was still alive when his wife came back, and indeed it appeared that he might recover, for there was a bit of colour in his cheeks. Mabel tucked him up nice and cosy in his bed, wiped his nose, straightened his night-cap, and then went into the back kitchen to get on with her daily tasks. Soon the unmistakable smell of Welsh cakes on the griddle wafted into the bedroom, and Harold was greatly moved. "Mabel," he cried. "I smell fresh Welsh cakes on the stove! I think I could manage one or two!"

"Hush now, husband," came the reply. "You'll manage nothing of the kind, for those are for the funeral!"

The Narberth Assassins

In the bad old days before constables enforced the rule of law up in the Presely Hills, human life was cheap. An old woman from the back of beyond, not far from Mynachlog-ddu, decided that she could take no more from her drunken, bullying husband. So she saved up her pennies for the best part of a year and hid them in an old pot until she had enough to hire a couple of notorious assassins from down Narberth way.

By arrangement, the two men turned up at the lonely cottage on the moor one winter's day when the old man was away at Newport market. They received their instructions from the wife, hearing that the husband was due back on the track over the mountain shortly after dark. Then they went off to the mountain, found the old trackway and settled down behind a gorse bush to await the passing of their victim. They sat there in silence in the freezing cold as dusk turned to night. At last, with no sign of the old man, one weary assassin turned to the other and said "He's a very long time coming. I hope to God nothing unpleasant has happened to him."

Value for Money

Dai and Iorwerth Rhys were bachelor brothers running a small farm up in the hills near Brynberian, with a bit of contracting work and dealing on the side. One of their sidelines was the collection and disposal of fallen animals.

One sad day, Iorwerth fell under a tractor and was killed. After making the necessary arrangements for the funeral, Dai thought he had better let the world know, so he rang the "Western Telegraph" office in Haverfordwest.

"I want to put a Death Notice in the paper," he said. "How much?"

"Certainly, sir," said the young lady. "Minimum nine words, and the cost is £5. What do you wish to say?"

"Put this: Iorwerth Rhys is dead."

"Very well," said the girl. "But you can have another five words for the same price."

Dai thought for a moment, and then, being a consummate businessman, he said: "You can add this: We also buy dead cows."

Rational To The Last

Henry Evans lived in Spittal with his wife and three sons. He was slipping away, and his family did not expect him to last the night. On the advice of the doctor, Smith Solicitor was summoned to the house in spite of the lateness of the hour, to help Henry to draw up his last will and testament. While the solicitor went to work with the dying man the family sat together in the parlour downstairs, comforted by the next door neighbours. The house was a small one, and they could hear everything that went on in the bedroom.

"State exactly what is owing to you," said the solicitor.

"Willie Thomas owes me twenty-seven pounds," answered Henry. "Tommy Jenkins owes me seven shillings and sixpence, Dai Jones owes me ninety-three pounds, Bobby Evans owes me a sack of spuds...."

"Good, good," exclaimed Henry's wife to the listening neighbours. "His head is clear as a bell, and he's rational to the last."

"Now then," continued Mr Smith. "I must know about all your debts."

"To Harry Reynolds I owe one hundred and ten pounds, to Williams Blacksmith I owe fourteen shillings...."

At this the prospective widow leapt to her feet and ran to the foot of the stairs. "Don't listen to him any more, Mr Smith bach," she shouted. "Poor Henry's ranting and raving with the sickness, and it's clear his mind is gone!"

Premature Funeral at Mynachlog-ddu

One day around the year 1890 Dr Rowland Jones had to attend a funeral in the remote and beautiful hamlet of Mynachlog-ddu, in the hollow between the hills of Foel-drych and Talfynydd. The old and cantankerous wife of a local farmer had died, and although she had not been one of his patients Dr Jones felt obliged to go along to the funeral as a mark of respect for the family. There was a good turn-out at the church, and at the completion of the funeral service the bearers lifted the coffin onto their shoulders and made their way with measured tread down the aisle towards the church door. All eyes followed them, and there was as usual complete silence. But then there was a great thud as the corner of the coffin hit the door-post on the way out; upon which the lid flew off and up sat the "deceased" farmer's wife, very much alive. She was none too amused when she discovered that she had missed out on several days and a number of important events, including her own funeral. And she she was most put out when she realised that she was sitting in a coffin heading for the bottom of a very deep hole in the ground.

The burial was abandoned forthwith, and the assembled company dispersed with much talk of miracles on the lips of all and sundry. The old lady went back to her sick bed, where she remained for several more weeks. She made her poor husband's life a misery, for she refused to believe that a mistake had been made, and could not accept that both her family and her family doctor had declared her well and truly dead prior to her funeral and miraculous resurrection. However, her health deteriorated again, and once more she died. This time, very great care was taken to make sure that she really was a deceased person, and the funeral was duly rearranged.

On the appointed day there was an even bigger congregation at the funeral, and many strangers turned up out of curiosity. The service went off without a hitch, and once more the bearers raised the coffin onto their shoulders. Down the aisle they went, with measured tread. There was complete silence, and there was a great corporate holding of breath. Suddenly there was a theatrical whisper from the front row of the church, where the old farmer was sitting. "Now then, boys bach," he said to the bearers. "Take it nice and careful, and for God's sake mind the door-post!"

Conversation in Martletwy

One dull morning in Spring, an old farmer from Martletwy called at a neighbour's house. He was met at the door by his friend's wife, and the conversation went as follows, very slowly:

"Cold."
"Yes."
"Goin' to rain, I do declare."
"Yes."
"Is John in?"
"Oh yes, a's in."
"Can I see'n?"
"Nay."
"But I wants to see'n."
"Can't see'n. A's laid out."
"Why's a laid out?"
"A's died."
"Died?"
"Yes." Long pause.
"What was the matter with'n?"
"Nothin' serious."
"Sudden?"
"Yes."
"Very sudden?"
"Yes, very sudden." Long pause.
"Did a say anythin' about me cabbage plants afore a died?"

Spooky Night in the Graveyard

It was well past closing time, and the landlord of the "Rising Sun" had ejected the last of the late drinkers. Dai, Tommy and Jack stood in the darkness on St Thomas' Green having had just a few too many. "Goodnight, boys," said Dai. "I'd better be off home or the old woman'll murder me."

Knowing that he had to walk through the graveyard of St Thomas' Church on the way home to the bottom of town, Tommy said "Aren't you afraid, Dai, goin' home through the graveyard with the wind in the trees an' all them ghosts?"

"The devil I am!" replied Dai. "I'm afraid o' nothin' and I ain't never seen a ghost yet." And off he went, heading unsteadily homewards.

After he had departed Jack said to Tommy "Come now, Tommy. We'll give'n the shock of his life." They ran by a short cut along Hill Street, and reached the graveyard ahead of their friend. They found a newly opened grave, and Jack jumped into the bottom of it while Tommy hid behind an old yew tree. After a few minutes they heard the rusty gate swing as Dai entered the graveyard. He was whistling cheerfully as he came along the path towards the conspirators. At the appropriate moment Tommy suppressed his giggles and imitated an owl. Dai stopped and listened, then continued on his way. As he passed the open grave a deep moaning noise came from it. Addressing the noise, Dai shouted "What's the matter with thee?"

"Oh, woe is me! Woe is me! I cannot rest!" said the weird voice from the grave, and continued with its baleful groans.

"No wonder tha can't rest, tha poor bugger," said Day. "They forget to shut thee in nice and tidy! But never mind - I'll give thee a hand." And with that he seized the gravedigger's shovel and began to throw earth into the open ground, to the great discomfort of the temporary inhabitant. As he warmed to his task, Tommy emerged from behind his tree and Jack yelled like a stuck pig. It was only with difficulty that the friends managed to get Dai to stop his shovelling. Later on Jack crept back to his home in Portfield, somewhat the worse for wear and covered from head to toe in earth and embarrassment.

Nothing But The Best

It was a beautiful funeral, and with old Lizzie Jenkins safely laid to rest in the graveyard of Caersalem Chapel the assembled company retired to the home of the deceased. There were relatives and friends from far and wide, and soon (as is the way of things) the tears turned to laughter, and animated conversation filled the house. Being a Baptist household, alcohol was not much in evidence, and in any case most of the men had drunk too much at the wake the evening before; but there was an excellent spread of sandwiches, buns, bara brith and cup cakes, followed by trifle with just a modest dash of sherry in it. Soon the kettle had boiled, and nice cups of tea were handed out in all directions.

Rev Ifan Phillips was doing his best to keep up a conversation with some of the elderly ladies from the neighbourhood when old Lizzie's maid came up to him with a plate piled high with currant buns. "Here we are, Reverend Phillips bach," she said. "Just you have one of these buns. Nothing but the best here today. The corpse have baked them herself."

Value for Money

J.J. Morris the Cardigan Auctioneer was not too well, and for several days he went around town feeling very sorry for himself. He went to several of the local doctors to see if he could get the problem diagnosed, but got a different story from each of them. This did nothing for his peace of mind, and he became more and more depressed. A few days later he met his old friend Harold in the Guildhall in Cardigan, and mentioned his medical problem to him.

"Don't you worry, JJ bach," said Harold. "I have a friend in Cardiff who is better than those blokes on Harley Street. He can take a look at you, and what with all these scientific techniques he will have your trouble sorted out in no time at all."

"Sounds as if that might be a good idea," mused the auctioneer. "How much will it cost?"

"Normally fifty guineas, but for you I can probably arrange things for a price of twenty-five."

"Twenty-five guineas!" exclaimed Mr Morris. "Good Lord! I've already got a better bid than that from Jones Undertaker!"

Made to Last

David Parry had just died, and his wife had the sad task of organizing things for the funeral. She ordered a coffin from Billy Box and then went down the street to Jones Draper to get a shroud. "Good morning, Mrs Parry bach," said Mr Jones. "There's sad I am to hear your news. Bad business indeed."

"Thank you, Mr Jones bach," said Mrs Parry. "Grateful I am for your condolences. Now then, I have come to get a shroud for the dear departed. What will it cost me?"

"Seven and sixpence. Top quality - guaranteed to last a lifetime."

"Seven and six! But, Mr Jones bach, I can get one for five bob at Jenkins Siop Fach."

"That may be," said Mr Jones haughtily, "but you gets what you pays for in this world. I have some experience of Mr Jenkins' shrouds, and you can take it from me, Mrs Parry bach, that if you gets one from him the corpse will have his knees through it in a week."

A Lapse of Memory

The trouble with all these Dai Joneses in Pembrokeshire is that it gets a bit confusing at times. This particular Dai Jones came from Newport, and had a tendency to have a few too many. One Saturday night in the middle of summer he had a good evening in the "Golden Lion" and was heading home somewhat the worse for wear. He got as far as St Mary's Churchyard before his endurance gave out on him. He staggered in through the gate, carefully hung up his jacket nice and tidy (as he always did, through force of habit), and then stretched himself out on a convenient slate slab and went to sleep.

When he woke up the sun was shining brightly, the birds were singing, and there was the smell of buttercups in the air. Dai thought he must be in heaven, and this was confirmed when he raised his head and saw a tombstone with his jacket on it. On the tombstone there was an inscription which read: "Here lies the body of Dai Jones."

"Well well, there's nice it is in Heaven," he said, closing his eyes and listening to the birds. "But there's a funny thing for you. I don't remember the first thing about the funeral."

Chapter Fourteen

PEMBROKESHIRE NICKNAMES

In Pembrokeshire there are too many Evanses, Joneses, Hugheses, Williamses and Thomases. It is not surprising, therefore, that nicknames have to be used to distinguish one person from another. The tradition of using nicknames is, of course, very old and such names are by no means restricted to those with the commonest surnames. Here are few of the most original:

Evans the Death was (of course) a local undertaker.

Dai Loco was a GWR engine driver.

Barry Central Eating had one tooth in the centre of his mouth.

Georgie One Ball had suffered an unfortunate accident.

Mrs Giggle Jenkins was renowned for her good humour.

Morgan Mafeking's auntie once went on a holiday to South Africa.

Mavis Milkwood was well known for her amorous adventures in the local wood.

Casey Holy Father was an Irishman, and devout Roman Catholic, and father of twelve children (at least).

Edith Small Change never had enough money in her pocket to pay for her groceries.

Davy Seven Waistcoats was a Prendergast waggoner who liked to dress well to keep out the cold.

Joe Booty was a member of the rag and bone fraternity.

Bobby Babel Tower is reputed to be fluent in three different languages.

Quick Dick was a Haverfordwest street cleaner renowned for his speed about the town.

Thankyou Ta was a Haverfordwest shop-keeper well known for the words which he always used on completing a transaction.

Bronwen Bosom was well endowed, and made sure that the whole world knew about it.

James the Filth was a respectable God-fearing newsagent whose wholesaler once sent him - in error - a parcel of girlie magazines.

Unconscious had a tendency to drink too much on a Saturday night.

Tom Never Stop was always in too much of a hurry.

The Missing Link was not renowned for his delicacy, good looks or table manners.

The Frog Man has the good fortune to live in a house called Pwll y Broga (pool of the frogs).

Peter Rabbit is a well known hotelier who once ran a rabbit-breeding business.

Dai the Ghost usually looked more dead than alive.

Dai Eighteen Months had one complete ear and one half ear.

Will Population was the father of thirteen children.

Dai Mikado once sang a very small part in a Gilbert and Sullivan opera.

Cosmic Jack, when he was young in the far-off Flower Power days, had a habit of saying "Cosmic, man!"

Willie Bingo once had the misfortune to win a pound at a bingo game.

Jack the Bomb was an early member of CND.

Dai Quiet Wedding is reputed to have worn gym shoes on the occasion of his marriage.

Dai Upper Crust is a local baker who once shook hands with a member of the royal family.

Horizontal Harry was a boxer who never made the grade.

Doctor Strangelove was a local GP who specialized in gynaecology and extra-marital affairs.

Mrs Dai Double Yolk was an egg merchant's wife who gave birth to twins.

Ned Bakerloo once lost his way on the London underground.

Toni Titanic weighed 20 stones.

Colin Compensation once made a profitable insurance claim after writing off his car in a crash.

Aaron the G-string went away to Cardiff, where he became the proud owner of a strip club.

Casanova Morris, unhappily married, advertised under a pseudonym for a female companion, and got only one reply - from his wife.

Dai Bananas was the nickname used in Pembrokeshire for Sir David Maxwell Fyfe, the Minister for Welsh Affairs.

Tom Twice had the misfortune to be christened Thomas Thomas.

Dai Foot-and-Mouth used to support the Narberth rugby team, and was well known for exhorting the forwards, in a voice of thunder: "Feet! Feet! Feet!"

Eddie Click Click was a Carmarthen photographer often seen in Pembrokeshire.

Two-foot Jones once worked in the two-foot seam in Hook Colliery.

Owen One-I-Got never had more than one cigarette left in his packet.

Billy Never Never was reputed to have been celibate all his life.

Jones Halleluja got very worked up whenever he heard a good sermon.

Williams Messiah was one of many Pembrokeshire men to study at Jesus College, Oxford.

Dai Atomic went away to college to study nuclear physics.